COGNITIVE BEHAVIORAL THERAPY MADE SIMPLE

By

Daniel Anderson

TABLE OF CONTENTS

INTRODUCTION

We must have all experienced our hearts pounding very fast before a major job interview or when we are asked to make a speech before important personalities. We worry over family and financial problems or feel jittery at the prospect of meeting a date for the first time. If your worries and fears are preventing you from living your life in a normal way, you may very well be suffering from an anxiety disorder. Here we want to show you simple techniques you can use to prevent and overcome anxiety. These techniques have been reported as indeed panic attacks and anxiety cures.

You are free to take the techniques seriously and stop swallowing dangerous panic attacks medication in order to completely eliminate panic attacks from your life. I was once an anxiety and panic attacks sufferer. I missed several important job interviews because of this problem until I was able to find a permanent cure using the One Move technique. Before I used the One Move technique to cure my panic attacks and anxiety, these were the techniques - cognitive behavioral therapy and graded exposure therapy - that helped me overcome anxiety and panic attacks.

Cognitive behavioral therapy and graded exposure therapy are the two effective anxiety and panic attacks treatment techniques. The two techniques are actually behavioral therapy and they focus on behavioral modifications rather than on underlying psychological problems of the past. The two techniques took me between 5 and 20 weekly sessions.

Cognitive behavior therapy - focuses on your thoughts and behavior modifications. When used in panic attacks anxiety cures, cognitive behavioral therapy helped me identify and challenge the negative thinking patterns and irrational beliefs that are fueling my anxiety and panic attacks.

Graded exposure therapy - This technique helped me to confront my fears in a safe and controlled manner. Through repeated and graded exposures to the feared situations, I was able to acquire a greater sense of control of myself. As I was being made to face my fears without being harmed, my anxiety and panic attacks gradually disappeared.

I believe strongly that these techniques are the best approach to treating and eliminating the twin problems of anxiety and panic attacks. Even the medical world now agrees that the best treatment for anxiety disorder is through behavioral therapy. The One Move technique is an advanced from of behavioral therapy which I used to completely cure all my symptoms. This is a heart-warming news to all sufferers. Your panic attacks and anxiety can be cured without costly and dangerous antidepressant medications.

Feel confident and beautiful once more. Experience for yourself the immediate and fast cure for panic attacks and anxiety with the One Move technique.

How do you overcome Anxiety?

Steps to Overcoming Anxiety

With the aid of the lists below, you can successfully overcome anxiety;

Overcoming anxiety after it's developed into a major difficulty in your life can often be confusing and upsetting. However, anxiety disorders are very treatable problems.

This is a consumer guide for people who seek anxiety relief, but don't know how to get there. However, I suggest that everyone who seeks relief from chronic anxiety should review these steps, and complete any which you haven't yet done.

Step One:

Learn a little about anxiety disorders

Understanding how anxiety "works" is one of the keys to overcoming anxiety. Read my description of the different anxiety disorders and compare your experience with those descriptions.

Use the book to learn more about overcoming anxiety disorders. The purpose here is not to self-diagnose yourself - please consult a licensed clinician for a diagnosis - but to inform yourself as much as possible before you consult a clinician so that you can evaluate what a clinician tells you, be an informed consumer, and find effective methods for overcoming anxiety.

The internet is full of anxiety scams, so be wary! When something sounds too good to be true, it probably is.

It's common to experience some depression along with an anxiety disorder, and this is often a source of confusion to people. If this sounds relevant to you, read a little bit about depression.

Step Two:

Consult with your primary physician

A consultation with your physician is a must if you suspect you have panic attacks or generalized anxiety.

These symptoms can be caused by a variety of physiological disorders, and you should rule them out as part of the diagnostic process. You should certainly have one complete physical after the onset of these symptoms.

The other anxiety disorders don't generally require a physical, because there isn't any reason to think that they are caused by another physical ailment. However, you might still want to consult your physician, especially if you have a long history with that person. You might want his/her opinion about your situation; you might want a referral; or you might want to find out about possible medications you could use.

Be aware, however, that most physicians, because they specialize in various aspects of physical health, have very little training in the area of anxiety disorders. What training they do have, with respect to overcoming anxiety, is usually limited to medications. They may often be surprisingly unaware of cognitive behavioral treatment for anxiety disorders, even though it is generally regarded as the treatment of choice. When it comes time to seek professional help for overcoming anxiety disorders, you will probably need to go elsewhere.

If you don't have panic attacks or generalized anxiety, and have no other reason to consult your physician about overcoming anxiety, then skip ahead to Step Three.

Before you call for an appointment, make some written notes of what you want to discuss with your physician. The doctor's staff will probably ask you why you want an appointment; tell them that you've been having some problems and summarize them, briefly.

Many people have a fear of doctors, and have trouble making an appointment. This is a phobia, and will generally respond to the same CBT approach, once you decide that a visit to the doctor, however anxiety provoking, is in your best interest.

What to Expect from Your Physician

Your physician should listen to your symptoms, review your history, ask questions, and offer feedback and recommendations for overcoming anxiety. Since most physicians are trained principally in physical health and medicine, there is no reason to expect him/her to be an expert in anxiety disorders. However, your physician should take your complaints seriously, evaluate them, and offer suggestions for finding additional help.

If you are having panic attacks and have never been tested for thyroid malfunction, for instance, you should receive such a test, because thyroid problems can sometimes cause a person to have panic-like symptoms. If your symptoms resemble those associated with mitral valve prolapse, you should probably have an echocardiogram to evaluate that possibility. There are numerous physical conditions which can produce panic symptoms, and your physician should evaluate you for those possibilities if that has never been done before.

However, if you have had those tests before, and your doctor assured you that you were in good health, do not push for continual retesting! Many people do this because they hate the idea that they may have an anxiety disorder, and instead hope to find a physical problem. You can waste lots of time and money this way.

One set of tests is generally enough. If you need a second opinion for a particular reason, then get one. If you get more than two sets of tests, seriously consider the possibility that you are getting diverted from your task of overcoming anxiety!

Let's suppose that you've had a good consultation with your physician, the appropriate tests have ruled out any physical ailments which could be causing your symptoms, and you want to get professional help with overcoming anxiety. Now you're ready for step three.

Step Three:

Learn about the available treatments

There are basically two kinds of treatment which clinical research has shown to be effective in overcoming anxiety disorders: cognitive behavioral treatment (CBT) and certain forms of medication. Other forms of psychotherapy are often helpful in resolving some of the issues associated with anxiety disorders, but are generally not regarded as capable of resolving the primary problem. Which form of treatment should you choose?

My view is that most people with anxiety disorders are best served by trying a cognitive behavioral treatment first, and seeing what kind of results you get from that. You can always try medication later, if the CBT doesn't provide all the results you seek.

There are three principal reasons to try CBT first. First, unlike medication, CBT has no side effects. Second, the use of medications tends to lead a person to believe that he or she is now "protected" from anxiety disorders, and the sense of being protected often leads an anxiety sufferer to feel more vulnerable in the long run. Third, the results you get from CBT treatment will generally be much more long lasting than those you get from medications. Results from medication treatments tend to fade after the medications are withdrawn.

Some patients will need medication in addition to CBT, and some will not, depending on the severity of their condition and their particular diagnosis. Medication is nothing to be avoided if it seems necessary. However, I do believe it's true that in our culture, medications are overprescribed for these problems. This can be avoided if you start with CBT first.

The Anxiety Disorders Association of America website includes an overview of medications used to treat anxiety disorders

There are new forms of CBT in development, often labeled as "Third Wave" therapies. One in particular, Acceptance and Commitment Therapy (ACT) is quite useful in the treatment of Panic Disorder and other anxiety disorders. In my work, I blend methods from both traditional CBT and ACT, and find them both very useful in overcoming anxiety disorders.

Do I Need "Treatment" at All?

You may be wondering if you really need to see a professional, or if you can't just solve this problem on your own. In general, the more difficulty you are having, the more you may need professional help, but only you can decide how urgent your need is. Certainly there are many good sources of self help information you can use in overcoming anxiety disorders. If you choose to try anxiety self help, I suggest you follow a few guidelines.

* Get a "buddy", a coach, or a support person, with whom you can discuss your efforts on a regular basis. They don't have to be an expert. A major benefit is that, by telling someone of your efforts, you will find it easier to monitor your progress and hold yourself accountable. It's easy to forget about all your good intentions when you keep them to yourself.

* Follow an organized plan. Find a good self help book which pertains to your problem, and make that the basis of your work. If you have panic attacks and like the approach you find on this website, then try my Panic Attacks Workbook. If your problem is more about chronic worry, take a look at my book for chronic worriers, The Worry Trick.

* Evaluate your progress at regular intervals, at least monthly. After six months, re-evaluate your progress. If you're satisfied you're making

reasonable progress toward overcoming anxiety, continue on course. If you're not, consider seeking professional help at that time.

What about Group Treatment for overcoming anxiety?

Among the advantages of group treatment for overcoming anxiety are lower cost and the opportunity to share experiences with others who can relate to your situation. This can be particularly important for people who feel especially ashamed and imagine that they are one of a very few who suffer in this way.

I don't really think there are any disadvantages to a well run group treatment, although many people shy away from it because they believe they would pick up more fears from hearing other people's problems. In my experience in running groups, this has not been a problem and, while people are usually quite nervous before the first meeting, their anxiety is usually much lower by the end of the meeting.

Group treatments are often not available, so consider yourself fortunate if they are offered in your area. Your own personal preference is probably the most important deciding factor in the choice between group and individual treatment.

...And Support Groups?

You may also find it helpful to attend a support group. There are general purpose support groups designed to help people with a variety of psychological problems, and there are anxiety support groups which have a more specific focus - anxiety problems in general, or specific anxiety disorders such as Panic Disorder, Obsessive Compulsive Disorder, etc.

I think most people with a clearly defined anxiety disorder are better served by a support group which focuses specifically on their kind of problem, if such a group is available. However, there are also some good "general purpose" groups, such as Recovery International.

Step Four:

Identify Qualified Therapists

If you decide to get professional help, be prepared to do some work to find a good therapist. You can start by getting the names of therapists in your area who offer the kind of treatment you seek. The websites of the Anxiety Disorders Association of America and the Association for Behavioral and Cognitive Therapies offer a "therapist finder" section to help you find a specialist in your area. The sites for the Obsessive Compulsive Foundation and the TLC Foundation (compulsive behaviors such as hair pulling, skin picking, and nail biting) offer similar lists of professionals who specialize in those areas.

You will probably be better off if you can find a therapist who has specialized training and experience with the anxiety disorder for which you seek help. However, be aware that these lists will generally include any therapist who wishes to be included; they are not a licensing or accreditation process, simply a place to start. You still need to be an informed consumer.

Step Five:

Select a Therapist and Begin Treatment

An initial evaluation with a therapist may take anywhere from one to two sessions. It should enable the therapist to learn enough about you to give you some feedback about your situation and how that therapist proposes to help you, and should also give you a chance to ask more questions. One area you should certainly discuss with the therapist is what to expect in treatment, i.e., how will you know it is working? What would be a sign that it is not working?

You will probably also want to know how long treatment will take. What I tell new patients is that, while I can't immediately predict how long their particular situation will require, I do expect that they will have a gut feeling that we are moving in the right direction within the first month of weekly sessions, and that they should see some progress within the first two months. If this doesn't happen, it's a sign that something isn't working right, and we should figure out what's wrong.

CHAPTER ONE

COGNITIVE BEHAVIORAL THERAPY

The brain is a fascinating, time-saving beast. It has fast-tracked responses to certain situations so you don't even have to think about reacting, you just do. This becomes a problem, though, when your automatic response is one of fear in situations where, in reality, there's nothing to be afraid of.

It could be that you go into a state of panic every time you're called in to a meeting with your boss, because years ago, you lost your job in a similar way. Maybe you constantly overreact to innocuous comments from your other half, because you're scared they're going to leave you the same way your ex did. Or it could be that walking to the bus stop is riddled with anxiety thanks to your neighbour's Great Dane, which you believe will one day escape and attack you.

If you're tired of feeling this way, scientists say

you can retrain the part of the brain that's responsible for this reaction. It's called the amygdala, and it's an almond-shaped collection of neurons located in each side lobe of the brain.

"It's a part of the brain that occurs in animals and humans," Dr Fiona Kumfor, research officer at Neuroscience Research Australia, says. "So it's not this high level cognitive process that we associate with being human in terms of reasoning and thinking rationally. The amygdala is a very automatic part of the brain that helps us respond to our environment and it seems to be important for registering emotional information."

The brain is primed to quickly identify emotional stimuli, especially when we're in a dangerous situation, so that we can then act fast. "But in a modern lifestyle we're not really being confronted with tigers that we need to run away from". "Instead, it might be stress from work, or that you're never fully relaxed, and your body can then be in this hyper-aroused state where the amygdala is overworking. You might be interpreting emotional cues in the environment in a more exaggerated sense than needed."

Luckily, the brain is plastic and can be retrained. "Potentially, if we can retrain the amygdala, we can regulate these emotions so they're deployed in appropriate situations and not impacting on everyday life and mental health," Kumfor adds.

Shrinking the amygdala

A regular meditation practice of 30 minutes a day has been shown to reduce the size of the amygdala, allowing your rational thinking brain to take over, according to neuroscientists at Harvard University in the US. But which meditation is best? Associate psychologist David R Vago, from the Functional Neuroimaging Laboratory at Harvard Medical School, is an expert in the neuroscience of mindfulness. There are three practices that are best for a sustainable healthy mind.

The first is 'focused attention', where you concentrate on a single object, like a sound, the breath or how your body feels. The second is 'open monitoring', in which you become aware of your thoughts (see our example, right). The third is 'loving kindness', a traditional Buddhist practice in which you cultivate compassion – even for people you don't really like.

To try one of these approaches, do a search online for a guided meditation. Start small with only five minutes a day and slowly increase your practice time.

Unlearning the fear response

Another way to retrain the amygdala is through exposure therapy. As the amygdala is associated with fear, this approach can help those with anxiety, phobias, chronic pain or post-traumatic stress disorder, Dr Sylvia Gustin, senior neuroscientist at Neuroscience Research Australia, says. "In this technique we develop a fear hierarchy, which you then gradually work through to the most fearful situation," she explains.

The way it works is you list all the things that trigger your anxiety, then rank them in order of least to most unnerving. Rather than avoiding all these situations (which would mean the amygdala isn't retrained so it remains overstimulated) you start by exposing yourself to the smallest trigger. Once you're comfortable with that, you work your way up the list so that you can unlearn the fear response.

Quietening the anxiety

When therapy is combined with mindfulness, it can have even better results. A small-scale US study of war veterans with post-traumatic stress disorder found that those who completed group therapy along with mindfulness training showed a shift in their brain activity. The University of Michigan Medical School researchers found the areas of the brain in the regions that dealt with threats, including the amygdala, weren't as active as they previously were

Gustin is also an advocate of mindful practices, like yoga, to help decrease the activity of the amygdala, but acknowledges that strong anxiety can make it hard to focus. In those cases she says to be patient and stick with it: "We only heal ourselves when we treat ourselves nicely."

Do this daily

Psychotherapist Dr Timothy Stokes says this 'open monitoring' practice is ideal for retraining the amygdala: "The most powerful therapeutic tools begin with observing our thoughts and feelings. This practice creates an observer who watches and allays the tendency to get hijacked by problematic thoughts and feelings."

1. Imagine a situation that causes you anxiety or usually leads to you losing your cool, making the image as vivid as possible.

2. Pay attention to the emotions this causes. It could be an unsettled stomach, a sad feeling in your chest or a burning feeling in your torso.

3. Say to yourself: "This energy is just a feeling in my body."

4. Repeat steps one to three for up to 30 minutes.

4 things to do when anxiety strikes

Follow these steps from meditation expert and Zen teacher Diane Musho Hamilton…

1. Stay present Notice how your body is responding to the situation or perceived threat you're encountering.

2. Let go of the story Empty the mind of thoughts and judgement. This will break the loop between the mind and body.

3. Focus Is part of your body tight, shaking or painful? Focus on these sensations without trying to control or change them.

4. Breathe Aim for a consistent series of rhythmic, smooth and even breaths. This will allow you to centre yourself.

Still anxious? Try this...

Tapping

Tap your temples, cheeks or shoulders repeatedly until you calm down. The mild brain stimulation from the tapping helps to erase the physical basis for a fear memory in the amygdala, a study published in the journal Traumatology found. It doesn't matter if you tap one side or both. You can also try this the day before a stressful event.

Basking in blue

Picture the amygdala inside your skull. Now imagine it's glowing with soft blue light. Visualise the healing light pouring into your frontal lobes and gently setting off billions of neural pathways. This should help you better control your response to the situation that's causing the panic and foster a sense of calm.

Imagining a feather

Close your eyes and use your mind's eye to imagine a feather gently tickling the surface of your amygdala. This will help minimise the fear or anxiety you're feeling and stimulate a series of positive responses from the brain instead.

Proven Tricks For Overcoming Anxiety And Fear

Back in the earlier days of evolution, humans were prey to giant hyenas, cave bears, and predatory kangaroos.

We've been able to outlast those guys, but evolutionary psychologists will tell you that we're still on constant lookout for the thing that wants to eat us next.

The trouble is, the audience at your next presentation is not, in fact, a bunch of razor-toothed animals. They generally want to see you do well.

Since being plagued by anxiety is a sure way to sabotage your own success, we've put together a collection of research-backed tips for overcoming your fears.

Breathe deeply because it lets your nervous system know that it can chill out.

You've probably heard that breathing is a good call if you're stressed out.

But what's fascinating is the reason why it works so well.

"Deep diaphragmatic breathing is a powerful anxiety-reducing technique because it activates the body's relaxation response," explains Psych Central editor Margarita Tartakovsky. "It helps the body go from the fight-or-flight response of the sympathetic nervous system to the relaxed response of the parasympathetic nervous system."

Slowly expose yourself to the things you're afraid of, so they're no longer unfamiliar to you.

If you're trying to get comfortable with negotiating, speaking in public, or other scary activities, psychologists often recommend exposure therapy.

Rehab Institute of Chicago neuroscientist Katherina Hauner has found that it can dramatically improve the way people relate to their fears.

"It is usually done in a series of hierarchical steps, starting with a relatively low level of engagement with the feared situation, and increasing the level with each step," she told the Huffington Post.

"For exposure therapy with a dog phobia," she says, "we might start with just looking at a very small puppy from many feet away, and eventually work our way up to petting a very large dog."

Recognize when you're succumbing to 'misplaced' anxiety, and let it go.

As Wharton research scholar Jeremy Yip has

found, fear about one thing in your life has a way of spilling over into other parts of your life.

If you have car trouble on your way to work, there's a good chance that feeling of anxiety will carry over into your workday.

You might feel less confident about pitching your boss on a new project because when you ask yourself, "How do I feel about this?" your general feelings of anxiety make you more risk-averse.

To deal with that, try and recognize where the fear is coming from. If you're worried because you need to make improvements, listen to that. If you're worried because your exhaust is making funny noises, don't.

Spend time with your friends — social support reduces anxiety.

Three decades of research shows that people with close friends are better able to survive divorces, job losses, and other traumatic events.

"Friendfluence" author Carlin Flora says that friendship has long been an evolutionary advantage.

"When we lived in groups where survival itself was difficult, you needed someone who would be guaranteed to throw you a lifeline," she told Thought Catalog. "You can easily theorize that the notion of a best friend developed because we needed someone where we were number one on their list and they were number one on our list in those life and death situations."

Exercise to protect yourself against the effects of stress, which include anxiety and fear.

Working out helps people feel better.

The Mayo Clinic says that exercise helps release anxiety in three main ways:

• Exercise releases brain chemicals associated with easing depression, like endorphins.

• Exercise enhances your immune system, lessening the chance of depression.

• Exercise increases body temperature, which helps people calm down.

And a pro tip: If you're new to working out, psychologists say that "taking away the choice" of whether you're going exercise is the key to sticking to a workout plan.

Reframe anxiety as excitement so that you can devote more energy and resources to the situation.

Harvard Business School assistant professor Alison Wood Brooks has found that the best way to work with anxiety isn't to keep calm — but to get excited.

Emotions happen at two levels: There's the physical sensation, called arousal in the psych world, and then the way you mentally interpret it, called valence.

When you're anxious, your heart rate goes up — that's high arousal. And you read it as bad news — that's a negative valence.

The takeaway: If you're anxious, reframe it as excitement, since you can stay in that high arousal state but read it as good news instead. In experiments, that tactic makes people better public speakers and karaoke singers.

Prevent yourself from always focusing on the

negatives by looking at the big picture.

Here's a simple, age-old exercise from Swiss psychiatrist Paul Dubois. Every night, grab a piece of paper and draw two columns. List the things that troubled you in one, and things that were favorable in the other. Make at least one favorable entry for each troubling one.

The realization that you have good things happening every day helps prevent you from just thinking about the negatives.

A few times every day, recognize that at this very moment you're doing OK.

Neurospsychologist Rick Hanson says in his Psychology Today column that our humaninstincts of survival make us constantly unsettled and fearful, protecting us against ever completely letting our guard down.

But it's all a lie, according to Hanson. Your brain is automatically telling you something bad is going to happen, which may be true in the future, but not right now. By reminding yourself that you're OK right now, you can more easily settle your fear and build well-being.

Realize that not everything is the end of the world; one way to do this is by consciously trivializing tasks.

Social psychologist Susan K. Perry suggests in her Psychology Today column that you always think of yourself as playing. If something goes wrong, you can just try again, or try it in some other way.

And when you compare something in your daily life to decisions that are truly life-and-death, it gives you better perspective as to what's really important — and that failure at something that's probably just trivial isn't something to be so fearful or anxious about.

CHAPTER TWO

EXERCISES DESIGNED TO DEAL WITH ANXIETY

How a person deals with other human beings is a big factor in whether or not he or she succeeds in business and life. It involves emotional intelligence (EI), or the ability to recognize and appropriately react to feelings in yourself and the people around you, particularly when it comes to handling stress and frustration. According to Gustavo Oliveira--a consultant who has helped about 2,000 people worldwide improve their EI using something called The DeRose Method--it's a skill everyone can sharpen. Here are his words on four ways to build your emotional intelligence.

Study yourself.

To get a better understanding of your emotional responses, behaviors, and where your weaknesses may lie, learn to pay attention to your reactions and behaviors. And ask people close to you--only if they'll be honest--to tell you what areas of your personality need work.

Manage emotions during stressful situations by breathing correctly.

Deep and steady breathing through the nose with a relaxed ribcage is one of the best ways to lower stress in the body, and strong medicine for anxiety, fear and anger. Deep breathing sends a message to your brain to calm down and relax. The brain then sends this message to your body, resulting in a lower heart rate and blood pressure. And when you are relaxed and calm you can better manage your immediate emotions.

Channel your emotions.

One powerful method of handling negative emotions is to transform negative energies into positive ones by redirecting them to fuel new opportunities. For example, in 2009 I was expanding two successful businesses. Two years later, both had failed and my money was gone. I was crushed, frustrated and disappointed, but instead of letting my emotions reinforce an unproductive mindset and behaviors, I took a five-hour drive and started thinking about ways I could channel the power of frustration into something positive. During this time, I realized that my failures actually taught me many valuable lessons on how to run a business and the things that must be avoided. I decided to teach these lessons to others and created a course which was a huge success and became an amazing new asset.

Transmute your emotions.

Try to transform negative feelings such as anger, hatred, pain, and jealousy into positive ones such as, love, admiration, compassion and kindness. For example, I had a student who was a professional stand-up paddle (SUP) athlete and would become emotionally unstable every time a competitor provoked him during competitions, which would negatively impact his performance. So, I created a behavioral training response for him: I asked him to smile at the competitor, row harder and intensify his focus. With time and training his response improved drastically and his new and unexpected behavior destabilized the competitors who provoked him.

Envy is another common negative emotion. Some of my students have admitted that the achievements of others make them feel as though if they are not good enough. I train them to transform the feeling and substitute it with admiration for the person's success. They come to see it as an opportunity to learn from the person's strengths, which is a more useful and productive response.

Anxiety Disorders Treatment - Phobias

Most anxiety disorders are readily treatable with a combination of psychotherapy and medication. Learn the details of these treatments and other treatment options for generalized anxiety disorder, panic disorder, agoraphobia, social phobia, specific phobia, and post-traumatic stress disorder/acute stress disorder. Treatments for anxiety depend upon the specific disorder diagnosed by a trained mental health professional. Below you will find some general treatment guidelines for different Anxiety Disorders.

This document deals with the treatment of Phobias (fears). Other available documents deal with the treatment of Panic-Related Anxiety (including Agoraphobia), Trauma and Generalized Anxiety

Social Phobia

Social phobia is the most common anxiety disorder in the population. Both men and women experience it equally. The greatest single fear that exists for people is the fear of giving a public presentation or talk, which is a symptom of social phobia. This is because at the root of social phobia is the excessive fear of either being scrutinized by others or of performing a behavior out of anxiety in front of others that might be embarrassing or humiliating, such as speaking unclearly, trembling, or even blushing.

For those suffering from social phobia it can greatly affect the quality of their lives. Oftentimes, because of the extreme anxiety those with social phobia experience during interactions with others, they avoid many social opportunities. Some have had their career potential significantly thwarted if their career advancement has rested upon giving public presentations or developing career networking relationships. Others with social phobia struggle with feelings of loneliness because their social anxiety gets in the way of pursuing dating opportunities or they may avoid social gatherings such as parties.

Social phobia can often be confused with shyness. However, for the majority of those suffering with social phobia they tend not to be shy around those they are familiar with; they can even be quite outgoing when there is not the fear of making an impression on someone whose opinion of them is unknown. Also, those with social phobia experience an extremely high level of anxiety in social situations that far exceeds the discomfort that shy people experience in social situations.

Up until recently, not much was known or understood about social phobia, especially in terms of how to treat it. We now know that people who suffer from social phobia tend to misinterpret neutral social clues so that they think others are negatively evaluating them. They are also very concerned with making a positive impression on people because they greatly desire approval from others. They often doubt their own abilities to be able to be successful in making a good impression. Fortunately, we now have effective therapy interventions to treat those with social phobia.

Psychotherapy

The treatment of choice for social phobia is cognitive behavioral therapy within a group setting called CBGT (cognitive behavioral group therapy). The ideal treatment group size for CBGT includes six patients and two therapists. This treatment relies on a triad of cognitive behavioral interventions, which include: simulated exposures to feared situations through role-plays, cognitive restructuring, and homework assignments done in in vivo exposure.

Before group treatment begins, the patient meets with the therapist and a rank-ordered hierarchy of the patient's most to least feared social situations is constructed. The group creates simulated scenarios in which the patient is exposed to his/her least feared social situations and as the patient is able to conquer these scenarios, moves up on his/her hierarchy list. If the patient begins to feel anxious or increased physiological arousal during a simulated situation, the patient is taught to use a variety of relaxation techniques, such as deep breathing to reduce the anxiety. It is through these simulated exposures that patients are able to face their fears and work through them in a monitored, safe setting.

The second component of CBGT is cognitive therapy. This is very effective since researchers have discovered that social phobia is largely born out of irrational beliefs that people develop over time. The cognitive beliefs of someone with social phobia are based upon the possibility of being negatively evaluated by others, which leads to strong feelings of vulnerability. Also, because those with social phobia tend to have a strong need for approval from others, they fear that they lack the self-esteem, social skills, or ability to make a good social impression on people.

During the first few sessions of CBGT the therapist educates the patients about cognitive therapy and how they can learn to replace their irrational beliefs that lead to anxiety or fear with healthy beliefs. Throughout the simulated scenarios, the group members can then challenge each other's irrational beliefs. By being able to point out to a group member during a simulated exposure that the member's self-perception about how they are coming across in a social situation is distorted, it offers important cognitive restructuring in the moment. CBGT is a careful balancing act between exposure and periods of cognitive restructuring.

The third component of CBGT is having the patients carry out in vivo homework assignments. This means that once the patient has mastered a feared scenario in the group setting, that the patient then goes and exposes himself/herself to a real-life similarly feared scenario, such as giving a presentation or going to a party. This allows for the skills that the patient learns in the group to be transferred to real-life situations.

There are many advantages that the group setting offers to those suffering from social phobia as compared to receiving individual therapy. First, those with various degrees of social phobia can learn vicariously through each other how to effectively handle their fears in social situations. Second, it helps group participants to realize that there are other people with similar fears and problems. This realization helps to reduce participants' fears that their problems are unique and mysterious. Third, by participating in a group treatment it helps to strengthen the patient's public commitment to change. Fourth, a group offers multiple partners with whom role-plays can be practiced. Fifth, a group offers a range of participants who can provide invaluable feedback to each other to help challenge the participant's irrational beliefs underlying their anxiety.

Since a person with social phobia has usually been struggling with the disorder for many years, 3 months of CBGT is not going to completely rid a person of social phobia; however, a reduction in the patient's symptoms should be evident. If after the twelve weeks of CBGT the patient's social phobia has not improved, then it is recommended that the patient continue either in another CBGT group and/or receive individualized psychotherapy treatment. If the person's anxiety within the feared social situations is severe enough to produce panic attacks, then panic control techniques and education about panic attacks should supplement the person's treatment. (See treatment for panic disorder). If the person really does have weak social skills, then social skills training as a supplemental treatment intervention would be quite helpful. Another treatment alternative to try after engaging in CBGT is psychotropic medication.

Medication

Medication for social phobia should be considered as a second line treatment after effective cognitive behavioral treatment has been attempted. Some medications can be helpful in the treatment of someone with social phobia in which cognitive behavioral therapy has been unsuccessful. The medications that have proven to be most successful in treating social phobia are the antidepressant medications called MAOIs (monoamine oxidase inhibitors), such as phenelzine (Nardil). The MAOIs seem to work best for generalized social fears. However, taking MAOIs requires many dietary restrictions because certain foods containing the pressor amine, Tyramine, such as the majority of cheeses, alcoholic beverages, and yeast products can produce an adverse reaction with the medication causing dangerously high blood pressure.

For more specific forms of social phobia such as public speaking and performance anxiety the beta-blockers, such as atenolol have been successful. These provide the convenience of only having to take them just a few hours before the specific anxiety provoking event. However, these medications have not proven to be very successful for severe generalized social phobia.

Recently, the SSRI anti-depressant medication called Paroxetine (Paxil) has received attention for reducing the symptoms of social phobia. This medication generally has few side effects and can be taken for more severe generalized forms of social phobia.

Specific Phobia

Specific phobias are the most prevalent anxiety disorders within the population. They occur when a person develops an irrational fear to a specified object or situation and feels a great degree of anxiety or even has a panic attack when exposed to that feared object or situation. Approximately five to twelve percent of the population has a specific phobia with slightly more women than men being affected by a phobia. Phobias that develop during childhood are usually outgrown by adolescence. Most specific phobias develop during adolescence or adulthood in a person's mid-twenties.

A phobia can develop in a person at anytime as a reaction to a traumatic incident. For example, if a person is in an accident that occurs on a bridge the experience may create a phobia of bridges. Sometimes people can develop a phobia by witnessing something bad happening to another person. For example, witnessing a person being bitten by a snake might create a phobia of snakes in the person who witnessed the incident. People can also develop phobias from hearing about information that might frighten them, such as a person who hears an in-depth story about a plane crash on the news might then develop a phobia of flying. People who have a specific phobia are aware that their level of fear and anxiety about the feared object or situation is unreasonable.

The most common subtypes of specific phobias are: animal, including animals and insects; natural environment, including bad weather, water, and heights; blood-injection-injury, including seeing blood from an injury, injection, or medical procedure; situational, including bridges, flying, using public transportation, and tunnels.

The most common situation that people fear most is actually public speaking. However a fear of public speaking is categorized under social phobia. This is because the primary feature of social phobia is a fear of being in a situation in which a person will be evaluated by others or somehow do something that will cause humiliation and/or embarrassment to oneself in public. Public speaking is more about the fear of being under public scrutiny, than fearing a specific situation based solely on irrational fears of that situation.

Specific phobias usually tend not to cause much disruption in a person's life. Most people are able to lead normal lives easily able to avoid whatever specific situation or object the person fears. For example, if a person has a phobia of snakes it is unlikely that being afraid of snakes will disrupt the person's life, unless the person is a forest ranger or works in the snake collection at a zoo. However, a specific phobia can become a problem for people who have to travel by plane regularly for business and have a fear of flying, or are afraid of elevators and have to use an elevator on a daily basis either for professional or personal reasons.

Fortunately, specific phobias are very treatable. The treatment of choice consists of cognitive behavioral interventions. Medication may be used in an adjunctive manner depending upon the severity of the phobia.

Psychotherapy As A Treatment

Psychotherapy is the treatment of choice for specific phobias. Cognitive behavioral treatment interventions including exposure, systematic desensitization, cognitive re-structuring, and relaxation techniques include the best approach to treat specific phobia.

Exposure therapy is the most effective therapy treatment technique for specific phobia. This intervention entails exposing the patient to the feared situations or objects for continuous periods of time. This way the patient is forced to confront his/her fears within the context of therapeutic management. The patient starts with situations that are the least anxiety provoking, such as seeing pictures of snakes, and works up through a hierarchy of gradually more difficult scenarios to most anxiety producing, such as holding a snake. The patient is taught a variety of relaxation techniques such as progressive muscle relaxation and deep breathing so that the patient can control anxiety levels during exposure to the feared object or situation.

Systematic desensitization is another widely used intervention for specific phobia. It involves having the patient imagine being exposed to the feared object or situation. Again, the patient begins with the least anxiety producing scenarios and works up to the most anxiety producing scenarios. The patient is encouraged to imagine very specific details associated with the feared object or situation such as smells, tastes, sounds, visual cues, and touch in order to make it as real as possible. Relaxation techniques are used to moderate anxiety levels. Studies have indicated that exposure to the feared scenarios in a person's imagination is an effective technique for conquering specific phobias.

Cognitive therapy is also helpful to people with specific phobia since their fears about a particular object or situation are based on irrational beliefs. Using cognitive therapy, the therapist helps the patient to identify what the irrational beliefs are that the person holds to be true about the feared object or situation. Then the therapist helps the patient replace the irrational beliefs with more realistic or adaptive beliefs about the feared object or place. Sometimes this may also require educating the patient with correct information about whatever it is the patient fears. For example, a person's phobia of flying may be fueled by not understanding how an airplane works and the extensive training that airline pilots have. By educating the patient with this information it can help the patient form more realistic beliefs that help reduce the patient's fear.

Medications As A Treatment

There are not currently any psychotropic medications used just to treat specific phobia. Medications should only be used as an adjunctive treatment approach if the person is experiencing moderate to severe anxiety or panic when in the presence of the feared object or situation. Another factor to consider is how often the person is confronted with the feared object or situation. For instance, if the person is phobic of elevators and must use an elevator every day for work then medication is more strongly indicated. Also, the use of medication will depend on whether or not the person is effectively able to reduce their anxiety with relaxation techniques.

If medication is indicated for a specific phobia than the anti-anxiety benzodiazepine agents such as Alprazolam (Xanax) or Clonazepam (Klonopin) would be the drug of choice. This is because they are short acting, which means they work quickly to relieve anxiety, so they do not have to build up in a person's body over time to be effective. Also, since they are short acting they leave a person's system quickly so that the person does not have to deal with ongoing negative side effects of being on a continuous medication.

It is important to use benzodiazepines carefully, however, because they are highly physically and psychologically addictive. They should not be prescribed to anyone who has any prior history of addictions and/or substance abuse. These medications need to be prescribed and used with caution.

CHAPTER THREE

FEAR IN THE BRAIN

Fear may be as old as life on Earth. It is a fundamental, deeply wired reaction, evolved over the history of biology, to protect organisms against perceived threat to their integrity or existence. Fear may be as simple as a cringe of an antenna in a snail that is touched, or as complex as existential anxiety in a human.

Whether we love or hate to experience fear, it's hard to deny that we certainly revere it – devoting an entire holiday to the celebration of fear.

Thinking about the circuitry of the brain and human psychology, some of the main chemicals that contribute to the "fight or flight" response are also involved in other positive emotional states, such as happiness and excitement. So, it makes sense that the high arousal state we experience during a scare may also be experienced in a more positive light. But what makes the difference between getting a "rush" and feeling completely terrorized?

We are psychiatrists who treat fear and study its neurobiology. Our studies and clinical interactions, as well as those of others, suggest that a major factor in how we experience fear has to do with the context. When our "thinking" brain gives feedback to our "emotional" brain and we perceive ourselves as being in a safe space, we can then quickly shift the way we experience that high arousal state, going from one of fear to one of enjoyment or excitement.

When you enter a haunted house during Halloween season, for example, anticipating a ghoul jumping out at you and knowing it isn't really a threat, you are able to quickly relabel the experience. In contrast, if you were walking in a dark alley at night and a stranger began chasing you, both your emotional and thinking areas of the brain would be in agreement that the situation is dangerous, and it's time to flee!

But how does your brain do this?

Fear reaction starts in the brain and spreads through the body to make adjustments for the best defense, or flight reaction. The fear response starts in a region of the brain called the amygdala. This almond-shaped set of nuclei in the temporal lobe of the brain is dedicated to detecting the emotional salience of the stimuli – how much something stands out to us.

For example, the amygdala activates whenever we see a human face with an emotion. This reaction is more pronounced with anger and fear. A threat stimulus, such as the sight of a predator, triggers a fear response in the amygdala, which activates areas involved in preparation for motor functions involved in fight or flight. It also triggers release of stress hormones and sympathetic nervous system.

This leads to bodily changes that prepare us to be more efficient in a danger: The brain becomes hyperalert, pupils dilate, the bronchi dilate and breathing accelerates. Heart rate and blood pressure rise. Blood flow and stream of glucose to the skeletal muscles increase. Organs not vital in survival such as the gastrointestinal system slow down.

A part of the brain called the hippocampus is closely connected with the amygdala. The hippocampus and prefrontal cortex help the brain interpret the perceived threat. They are involved in a higher-level processing of context, which helps a person know whether a perceived threat is real.

For instance, seeing a lion in the wild can trigger a strong fear reaction, but the response to a view of the same lion at a zoo is more of curiosity and thinking that the lion is cute. This is because the hippocampus and the frontal cortex process contextual information, and inhibitory pathways dampen the amygdala fear response and its downstream results. Basically, our "thinking" circuitry of brain reassures our "emotional" areas that we are, in fact, OK.

Similar to other animals, we very often learn fear through personal experiences, such as being attacked by an aggressive dog, or observing other humans being attacked by an aggressive dog.

However, an evolutionarily unique and fascinating way of learning in humans is through instruction – we learn from the spoken words or written notes! If a sign says the dog is dangerous, proximity to the dog will trigger a fear response.

We learn safety in a similar fashion: experiencing a domesticated dog, observing other people safely interact with that dog or reading a sign that the dog is friendly.

Fear creates distraction, which can be a positive experience. When something scary happens, in that moment, we are on high alert and not preoccupied with other things that might be on our mind (getting in trouble at work, worrying about a big test the next day), which brings us to the here and now.

Furthermore, when we experience these frightening things with the people in our lives, we often find that emotions can be contagious in a positive way. We are social creatures, able to learn from one another. So, when you look over to your friend at the haunted house and she's quickly gone from screaming to laughing, socially you're able to pick up on her emotional state, which can positively influence your own.

While each of these factors - context, distraction, social learning - have potential to influence the way we experience fear, a common theme that connects all of them is our sense of control. When we are able to recognize what is and isn't a real threat, relabel an experience and enjoy the thrill of that moment, we are ultimately at a place where we feel in control. That perception of control is vital to how we experience and respond to fear. When we overcome the initial "fight or flight" rush, we are often left feeling satisfied, reassured of our safety and more confident in our ability to confront the things that initially scared us.

It is important to keep in mind that everyone is different, with a unique sense of what we find scary or enjoyable. This raises yet another question: While many can enjoy a good fright, why might others downright hate it?

Any imbalance between excitement caused by fear in the animal brain and the sense of control in the contextual human brain may cause too much, or not enough, excitement. If the individual perceives the experience as "too real," an extreme fear response can overcome the sense of control over the situation.

This may happen even in those who do love scary experiences: They may enjoy Freddy Krueger movies but be too terrified by "The Exorcist," as it feels too real, and fear response is not modulated by the cortical brain.

On the other hand, if the experience is not triggering enough to the emotional brain, or if is too unreal to the thinking cognitive brain, the experience can end up feeling boring. A biologist who cannot tune down her cognitive brain from analyzing all the bodily things that are realistically impossible in a zombie movie may not be able to enjoy "The Walking Dead" as much as another person.

So if the emotional brain is too terrified and the cognitive brain helpless, or if the emotional brain is bored and the cognitive brain is too suppressing, scary movies and experiences may not be as fun.

All fun aside, abnormal levels of fear and anxiety can lead to significant distress and dysfunction and limit a person's ability for success and joy of life. Nearly one in four people experiences a form of anxiety disorder during their lives, and nearly 8 percent experience post-traumatic stress disorder (PTSD).

Disorders of anxiety and fear include phobias, social phobia, generalized anxiety disorder, separation anxiety, PTSD and obsessive compulsive disorder. These conditions usually begin at a young age, and without appropriate treatment can become chronic and debilitating and affect a person's life trajectory. The good news is that we have effective treatments that work in a relatively short time period, in the form of psychotherapy and medications.

CHAPTER FOUR

SUREFIRE WAYS TO GET RID OF BAD HABITS

Success, happiness and good health often elude us not because we lack good habits but because we have bad habits. Sometimes they are habits like procrastination or mindless spending. But at other times they can be addictions like smoking and gambling.

Knowing how our bad habits negatively influence our lives is rarely enough to break them. For example, all smokers are aware of the health consequences of smoking. Diseased lungs are displayed prominently in every cigarette pack. There would be no smokers in the world today if that worked.

This fails to work because we don't do our bad habits for the reasons we should not do them. No smoker has ever smoked a cigarette to get cancer. Students don't procrastinate to fail. So in order to break our bad habits, we must first remove the reason why we do them. In other words, we need to eliminate the desire to do the habit.

Once the desire is gone, it takes no willpower to break bad habits, just as it doesn't take willpower to not do things we have no desire to do. It doesn't take much effort to stop yourself from eating live frogs because you have no desire to do it. Breaking your bad habits can be just as effortless. You just need the right belief and the right system.

Our Habits Controls Us

From the outside, it would seem that our bad habits is a matter of choice. Smokers, for example, do make the choice of trying their first cigarette. But no smoker has ever made a decision that they will keep smoking for the rest of their lives. We often fall into the trap thinking we can stop whenever we want, only to realize that we no longer have any control. When we watch the first episode of a TV show, we end up binge watching multiple seasons at a stretch because we cannot stop ourselves. Every addict wishes inside that he had never started because life was fine before their addiction but now they are hooked and cannot enjoy life without satisfying their craving.

Researchers from National Institute on Alcohol Abuse and Alcoholism trained rats to press a lever to get a piece food. The researchers later electrified the floor so that when the rat walked to get the food, it received a shock. In a different experimental setting, the rat recognized the danger in the electric floor and would avoid it. But when the rat saw the lever, the habits took over and the rat would press the lever and go for the food and get electrocuted every time. The rat could not stop itself in spite of being aware of the danger because the habits were so strong.

Similarly, dieters find it hard to resist junk, smokers struggle to quit and students procrastinate on their assignments in spite of being aware of the consequences it has on their lives. Strong habits create an obsessive craving which makes our brain behave on autopilot even if there are strong disincentives like loss of job, health, reputation, family or home.

When We Use Willpower to Quit, We Fail

We usually try to break bad habits using willpower, which makes us feel we are making a sacrifice. A Harvard study showed the 12 month success rates of people who used the willpower method to quit smoking with no education or support was 6%.

When using willpower to quit, we find life extremely unpleasant and difficult and have to be cautious all the time to prevent relapse. This is because the desire to do the habit always remains inside us.

10 % of former smokers who abstained from smoking for ten years showed ongoing cravings even years later. 3 Mere abstinence does not mean we have broken our habit. It just means we don't allow ourselves to do our habit. A person who does not drink alcohol but who is constantly thinking about alcohol is not a non-alcoholic but is an alcoholic who does not let himself drink.

We see the benefits of breaking our habits but also believe it provides us with something which we are now depriving ourselves of. This makes us miserable, vulnerable and increases desire that begins to obsess us. We try to overcome this by not thinking about our craving but that only makes us more obsessed.

Believing our problems can be easily solved by doing our bad habits we begin to question our decision to break our bad habits. Finally, we accept defeat and cave in. This minor relapse makes us feel bad and we indulge in the very same habit that made us feel bad, to feel better.

We fail to break our bad habits not because we lack willpower but because we don't eliminate desire. Without desire, willpower is not required to stop, just as it doesn't take willpower to not do the things we have no desire to do.

Why Does Our Brain Form Habits If They Are Bad?

Habits is a way for the brain to save effort by making rewarding behaviour automatic. Without habits, you will have to relearn how to brush your teeth every morning. Habits are useful but the problem is our brain cannot tell the difference between good and bad habits. Behavior that gives us short-term rewards often becomes habits, even if they cause long-term harm. Overeating, procrastinating and smoking becomes habit easily because the rewards are instant and the pain comes later. Developing the habit of exercising is harder because the reward comes later.

Schultz from the University of Cambridge, trained a monkey named Julio to pull a lever when a shape appeared on computer screen. Pulling the lever gave Julio a drop of blackberry juice which made the pleasure centres of his brain light up. When his brain started craving for the juice, Julio was glued to the monitor like a gambler in a slot machine. If the juice arrived late or diluted, this craving would turn into anger & depression.

Charles Duhigg's book, "The Power of Habit" focuses on the 3 components of a habit. The first component is the trigger, which tells the brain to start doing a particular behaviour (shapes in Julio's monitor). The second component is the behaviour that is done (Julio pulling the lever). The third part is the reward for doing the behaviour (Julio's blackberry juice). The habit is formed when the brain starts to crave for the reward as soon as the brain sees the trigger. There is nothing programmed in our brains that makes us want to overeat or smoke. But over time we slowly develop a neurological craving for these things.

Break The Habit By Seeing The Reward As An Illusion

The first step to breaking your bad habit is identifying the reward.

What do you really get doing your habit?

If the rewards you think your habits provided were actually real, then you can break your bad habits, simply by switching your existing habit with a healthier behavior that provided the same reward. For example, if you eat junk at work for distraction, then you can break your habit simply by replacing eating junk with a healthier distraction that does not add to your waistline. This is the premise of the book "The Power of Habit" and this works well for weaker habits. But try telling a smoker to resist his urge for smoking when he is bored by entertaining himself on YouTube. He won't be a successful non-smoker for very long. This is because most rewards of our habits are illusions.

We often rationalize why we do our bad habits but all the reasons we use to justify our behaviour are an illusion, excuses, fallacies or based on myth. For example, smokers believe they need cigarettes to relax, relieve stress, to concentrate or to relieve boredom. But cigarettes do not give them any of this. If it did, they should be a lot more relaxed, focused and less bored than non-smokers.

Most of us brainwash ourselves in a certain way that keeps us doing our bad habits. Only by identifying what we think is the reward can we address and remove the myths we have about the reward. When we begin to see through the illusory rewards, we eliminate desire by realizing that there is nothing to give up.

What We Give Up When We Break Bad Habits?

What are we giving up when we break our bad habits? Well, most of the time you are giving up absolutely nothing.

We don't do our bad habits for pleasure. We do it to feel normal. This feels like pleasure. A drug addict feels miserable, anxious, stressed and angry when he is deprived of his drug. When he shoots up his drug, he gets relief from all the negative symptoms. The subsequent dose partially relieves the symptoms but also ensures that the addict goes through withdrawal again. This keeps the addict stuck in the vicious habit loop. Normal people do not experience the symptoms of the drug addict. When we look at this it is obvious to us that the symptoms the drug addict experiences are caused by the drug, not removed by it. But we fail to have the same understanding when it comes to our bad habits.

Our bad habits cause symptoms of craving that normal people don't experience. We do our bad habits to partially relieve the symptoms but it only keeps us stuck in the vicious habit loop ensuring we experience the symptoms of craving again.

Unlike drug addiction which might require a visit to rehab, the craving caused by most bad habits including alcohol and smoking can be killed immediately when the belief system is changed. If you are not entirely convinced that there is nothing to give up, you need to examine the rewards of your bad habits and see them for what they really are. Otherwise, you will feel craving and will have to use willpower to prevent relapse.

The 4 Illusory Rewards

If you think your habit provides any of the following 4 rewards, you probably have an illusory reward:

1. Relieves stress

2. Relieves boredom

3. Improves concentration

4. Relieves anxiety and gives confidence

We will address the common myths people have about each of these rewards which will help dispel the illusion.

Reward 1 - Relief From Stress & Relaxation

For many, habits provide relaxation and relief

from stress. We all have several things stressing us out. Not just big tragedies but relatively minor things like work deadlines. We do our bad habits to relieve this stress and the stress does seem to go away. But what has really happened?

Apart from the environmental stress, we experience additional stress because of the aggravation caused by craving. Bad habits relieve this portion of stress it created through craving. But our real-world stress like work deadlines continues to exist. When we do our habits we feel better able to cope with this stress because we temporarily don't have the additional stress caused by the craving to deal with.

A study has shown that we fall back into our habits when we are stressed because we feel less anxiety and more in control when we do our habits. People who have been sober for years relapse when a major life catastrophe happens like a death of a loved one or divorce. This is because of a failure to understand that alcohol does not relieve stress but only adds to the problem.

The habits that we fall back on during times of stress need not be bad. In a study, students who habitually ate a healthy breakfast continued to eat healthy during the stressful period of their exams. Whereas students who gained extra weight during their exams had a habit of eating unhealthy. Consciously engineering your habits is important so that your habits make you better and not worse during times of stress.

Reward 2 - Relief From Boredom

Some people do their habit because they are bored. Boredom is a frame of mind and not a physical condition that can be cured. Initially, we are bored. Now we are bored and engaged in self-destructive behaviour. Our bad habits do not cure boredom. It just creates a temporary distraction that allows us to forget that we are bored.

If our bad habits did relieve boredom, then why do we have to engage in it multiple times or do it for longer periods at a stretch?

Most bad habits rob us of our energy and make us more lethargic, putting us in a state of mind where we cannot do anything else. Instead of doing something when bored like how a normal person would, we lounge around, do our bad habit and feel more bored.

If you know someone who plays excessive video games or who spends hours in front of the TV, you will see they are not any less bored. They will be extremely tired and will feel like shit for wasting so much time.

Reward 3 - Helps Concentration & Removes Mental Block

If you think your bad habits removes mental blocks and improves concentration, then you are not alone. Some of the greatest artists of the world including Van Gogh and Beethoven were addicts. But curing addiction does not lower creativity because your genes do not change. It is just your craving that goes away. So what really happens?

A study done on 96 undergraduates showed a reduction in the student's ability to do tasks that required visuospatial memory, when they experienced craving for chocolate. In other words, craving negatively affected the student's ability to remember.

Our bad habits cause craving which creates a distraction that makes it difficult to concentrate. When we need to concentrate we do our habits to eliminate the distraction caused by our craving. We give credit to our bad habits for helping us concentrate when it was responsible for the distraction to begin with. People without bad habits will not have problems with concentration because they don't experience the craving.

Over time people who believe that their bad habits help them concentrate begin to believe that it removes mental blocks. After you do your bad habits, your block will still exist, but only now you will get the job done just like how anybody would have done it. But your bad habits get the credit for helping you get the work done.

Your bad habits provide no mental performance advantage and believing it does is based on fallacy and myth.

Reward 4 - Confidence & Anxiety Relief

We acknowledge the relief provided by our bad habit as it removes the small amount of emptiness and insecurity. But we don't acknowledge that this emptiness and insecurity are the symptoms of our bad habits in the first placek.

People who have had their bad habits for many decades have been in a perpetual state of anxiety and emptiness so their bad habits seem to be the only way to get confidence and a relief from this feeling. Our bad habits do not relieve the anxiety in our lives, it causes it. People without bad habits never feel this insecurity or anxiety, to begin with.

Freedom from the self-loathing and dependency is one of the biggest positive changes people see in their lives when they break their habits. They are more relaxed and confident after breaking their bad habits and are better able to deal with their anxieties if it is not gone altogether.

Relief From Craving is The Only Reward

Craving and withdrawal can make you insecure, irritable, anxious or agitated. Though there is no physical pain, it causes mental agony giving us a feeling that something is not right. For example, smokers believe that withdrawal is a physical trauma caused by not satisfying their craving. But eight hours after putting out the last cigarette, a smoker is 97% nicotine-free. This happens every night during sleep. Only during the day does he feel the need to smoke every hour to fix his craving. After three days of not smoking, a smoker is 100% nicotine-free. Yet smokers relapse because of craving after months of abstinence. The truth is withdrawal and craving is almost always psychological even for smokers & alcoholics.

We associate our bad habits with pleasure because we see them satisfy our craving, but don't see them causing it. Our craving is not cured by our bad habits but is caused by it.

We might have started doing our bad habits for many reasons, but the only reason why we keeping doing them is to feed the craving. Every time we do our habit, the craving is satisfied temporarily. This provides a temporary relief, putting us in a normal state of mind. But by doing our habit, we have set ourselves up to experience craving again in the future. The more we feed our craving, the more it takes to satisfy it. Smokers go from one cigarette to chain smoking fairly quickly.

What we really enjoy is not our bad habits but the feeling we get when our craving is satisfied. It is like putting on tight shoes just for the pleasure of taking them off. This is why by breaking bad habits, you are giving up nothing.

Hidden Drivers of Bad Habits

Alcoholics Anonymous (AA) have a concept called dry drunk, where alcoholics stop drinking but still remain angry, selfish and narcissistic. Our bad habits are often symptoms of some inner conflict. Things like anger, shame, loneliness, fear and hopelessness that makes people start doing their bad habits, needs to be addressed first. Until the flawed beliefs are fixed, we will always remain vulnerable to relapse. The habit of procrastination, for example, can be fixed only temporarily, if the underlying fear of failure is left unaddressed.

Bad habits are a way for our sub-conscious mind to avoid the real inner conflict that exists inside us. The inner conflict is either a bitter truth ("I am ashamed of my past") or a distorted assumption ("I screw up everything" or "I am better than everybody"). This inner conflict is never a mystery but we make it a mystery because acknowledging the truth is uncomfortable. It is easier to think we have no choice or control over our lives than it is to take responsibility for fixing it.

The best way to fix inner conflicts is through therapy which works by bringing our inner conflict to light causing them to vaporize like a vampire. The next best way is service. Helping others has helped AA members reduce their desire to drink. A study of 195 addicted adolescents showed that treatment showed substantial improvement when it was accompanied by service. 10 This works because love neutralizes shame and service to others reduce obsession and craving by eliminating the inner conflict. Helpfulness may not help break bad habits by itself, but it addresses the internal conflicts that create craving.

The System To Break Bad Habits

Now that we have addressed the core beliefs and issues that make us do our bad habits, let us look at the step by step system to break bad habits. With this system, you will be able to break any habit easily and effortlessly without using willpower.

Helping Others Break Bad Habits

Do not patronize the person you are trying to help, by telling them why their habits are bad. They already know this and don't do their bad habits for the reasons they shouldn't do it. They do their bad habits to feel normal.

Do not tell them breaking bad habits is easy as it will only irritate them. Give them the support and praise to keep them moving forward.

Do not force them to break their bad habits. Even

if they try, they will use willpower to quit and end up failing. Tell them that people who succeeded in breaking their habits did not use willpower but instead addressed their flawed beliefs. Tell them how their bad habits only remove their need to do the habit which is perceived as pleasure by the brain. But in reality, their bad habit do not give them anything.

When they start believing that they can break their bad habits, their mind will begin to open up and that is when they are ready to read this book. Mention that there is no pressure to break their bad habits. If they want to continue to do their bad habits after reading this book, they can.

Where To Go From Here

The key to making it easy to break bad habits is to make your decision final and certain. Don't worry whether or not you have broken your bad habit. Know that you have. Do not ever doubt your decision. Celebrate it. Withdrawal is entirely psychological and if you are sulking, it only means you have not addressed your belief systems yet. Revisit Steps 2 to 4 in the system.

Don't make the mistake of procrastinating and not applying what you have learnt. You can wait for as long as you want to break your bad habits but the right time will never come and your habits are not going to be any easier to break tomorrow.

Some people think their bad habits has not caused any problem yet, so it is not a big deal if they don't break their habits now. The best time to fix the roof is when it is not raining. Don't wait for things to go wrong before you fix your bad habits. Break your bad habits now.

CHAPTER FIVE

STRONGER FOR THE EXPERIENCE

Many of us don't realize how much our past is dictating our current and future lives. We think that we're being cautious and smart, that we're using hard-earned information from what happened long ago to avoid the same mistakes now.

Little do we realize that holding onto past occurrences just makes them happen again and again. In this book, I'm going to talk about why we hold onto the past, how it messes with our lives now, and how to let it all go.

The ego is the part of your mind that stays focused on the past. It has a really potent message about the past that it feeds you all the time, and that message is: Watch out, it's going to happen again.

This is one of the sly tricks of the ego; this belief alone is enough to keep you stuck. And it works like a charm.

The fear that what happened in the past is going to happen again makes us so scared that it keeps us from enjoying what is actually happening now. Instead of being open to different experiences and outcomes, we are riddled with fear that we are going to get hurt again.

When our minds are focused on something then it becomes our experience; our expectations become our realities. The reason this is true is because we cannot separate ourselves from our perception. What we perceive is what is real to us. If your perception is stuck on repeat in the past, then your present is repeating in the past too.

It isn't until we actually let go of the past completely that we can really move on and have a new experience. And the way to do that is by surrendering your fears.

You have to become willing to create a different reality. Your life will not turn out differently unless you do something different. And luckily, you can.

Here's how to let go of past fears that are cursing

you in the present:

1. Notice when your fear surfaces—the one that says, It's going to happen again.

If we are going to let go of fears we have to recognize them first. Just noticing goes a long way; it's called gaining consciousness.

When you start to feel yourself getting a little anxious or fearful, stop and take notice. Think to yourself, "Oh here it is, I'm starting to get freaked out."

This step helps you start to disengage from the fear as the ultimate reality. It helps you to realize that you are not your fear.

2. Call out the fear.

Get clear about what you are afraid of. What happened? What are you afraid of happening again?

Maybe the fear is that when you opened-up to another person, you felt rejected. Maybe the fear is when you got close to another person, you lost yourself.

Name it (I would even suggest writing it down). Again, knowing what the fear is is the only way you can let it go.

When fear flies under the radar, it has the power to plague us without us even knowing it. If we are constantly inundated with unconscious fears then we start to develop other symptoms-- illnesses, physical symptoms, depression, anxiety and other ailments.

If something feels "off," don't be afraid to investigate what's going on. You gain freedom by looking your fears in the eye.

3. Become willing to let the past go through forgiveness.

It always comes back to forgiveness because forgiveness equals letting go.

The things we are holding onto from the past are the things that we have not fully forgiven. They come in the form of resentments, but also just flat-out fears.

The essence of forgiveness is: I know that what happened was a mistake. I know that it happened because we (I, the other person, or both of us) were acting out of fear. I am willing to feel peace about it and let it go.

Big words. So important.

Forgiveness is a life-changing practice. It is absolutely crucial in creating a new reality in your present and future. For a detailed guide on the how to forgive, check out Why Forgiveness Will Change Your Life.

4. Recognize that peace lives in you.

Really. It does.

Often we want the people around us to mold and change so we can feel better. But actually if we are scared of the past (OUR past) then it's our job to regain a sense of peace.

Ideally the people in our lives will support us when we're scared, but ultimately it's not their job to make everything better. Once we realize this, then we stop relying so heavily on others to feel safe.

Prayer and meditation are great tools to bring

you back into the present. If you simply close your eyes, feel your breath, and listen to your heart, you can easily re-center and orient yourself back to now.

Fear is only activated when we are focused on the past or the future. Anytime you feel fear, if you can make your way back to now you will realize that you are actually safe and well.

The next time you feel fear coming on, implement all four of these steps. They will help you come back to who you really are, which is a peaceful, joyful, magnificent person.

Just remember, you are much more powerful than your fears; you don't have to keep living them over and over again. When you choose to have a different experience in life, that different experience will also choose you.

CHAPTER SIX

PRACTICING MINDFULNESS MEDIATION

To effectively manage stress and anxiety, you need to calm down your amygdala's fear and panic. A mindfulness mind-set and stress reduction techniques are the antidote to being swept away or immobilized by stress and anxiety. Practicing mindfulness for stress and anxiety is an open, compassionate attitude toward your inner experience that creates a healthy distance between you and your stressful thoughts and anxious feelings, giving you the space to choose how to respond to them.

With mindfulness practice for stress and anxiety, you learn how to sit peacefully with your thoughts and feelings in the present moment, creating an inner calm to help contain and reduce stress and anxiety.

If I had to pick just one tool for dealing with stress and anxiety, I'd choose mindfulness. The use of mindfulness is supported by a growing neuroscientific literature, demonstrating actual changes to neurons in the amygdala following mindfulness training. Mindfulness-based interventions have gained the attention of therapists, educators, coaches, and even politicians and business leaders. This brain skill can have far-reaching beneficial effects, not only transforming brain neurons but improving immunity, health, life, and relationship satisfaction. Mindfulness for anxiety and stress has the potential to make not only individuals but even businesses, institutions, and societies more stress-proof.

In this book, you'll learn about mindfulness, its history in ancient Buddhist philosophy, and the current use in the West of mindfulness exercises as a widely accepted and effective mind-body practice for anxiety and stress reduction. You'll learn the qualities of a mindful mind-set and how to train your mind to be more mindfulthrough mindfulness meditation practice and mind-set change. Read on, and learn why "The Mindful Revolution," as Time magazine dubbed it, is the key to managing your stress and anxiety!

The Roots of Mindfulness

Mindfulness is both a skill and an attitude toward living that originated thousands of years ago as part of Buddhist philosophy. According to the Buddha, mental suffering (or inner stress) occurs because we cling to positive experiences, not wanting them to end, and we strive to avoid pain, sadness, and other negative experiences. This effort to control our mental and bodily experiences is misguided and out of touch with the reality of living. We can never escape loss and suffering because these are natural parts of life. Our experiences are always changing. Living things wither and die, to be replaced by new living things. The forces of nature are beyond human control.

The Buddha believed that although pain is inevitable, suffering is not. Suffering results from our attempts to cling to pleasure and push away pain. Buddhist teaching describes suffering in terms of being shot by two arrows. The first arrow is the pain and stress that are an inevitable part of being human. These types of stressors, such as aging, illness, and death, are beyond our control. The second arrow is the one we use to shoot ourselves in the foot by reacting to the natural experience of human suffering (or stress) with aversion and protest. It's as if we've become phobic of our own emotions! When we begin to feel stressed, we create mental stories of worry and regret that compound our mental suffering. We get caught up in negative beliefs about ourselves, regrets about the past, or worries about the future, taking us out of the present moment. Or we try to push our feelings of stress and anxiety away through addictions and avoidance. These strategies just make things worse. As one of my wisest supervisors once said, "The cover-up is worse than the crime!" Practicing mindfulness for stress and anxiety returns us to the present moment.

The Buddha also believed that if we can understand the nature of suffering and learn to accept pain and loss with compassion (rather than running away from them), our mental suffering will lessen. We may not be able to get rid of the first arrow of inevitable pain and grief, but we can get rid of the second arrow of self-created mental and emotional suffering with mindfulness-based stress-reduction techniques. By looking at our own inner experiences with a curious, nonjudgmental, and welcoming attitude, we can learn to better tolerate negative states of mind (such as feeling stressed and anxious) and relate to these experiences in a more kind, accepting way. Using mindfulness for anxiety and stress, by calibrating us for momentary neutrality, creates space for such tolerance. Another truth about suffering that the Buddha understood is that our thoughts, feelings, and physical sensations, like all other aspects of life, are transient and constantly changing. When we directly face and accept negative experiences, they'll move through us, rather than getting stuck. The Buddha also believed that living a life of peace, self-discipline, service, and compassion would create an end to suffering on a higher level.

University of Massachusetts Medical School professor emeritus Jon Kabat-Zinn was the visionary who first introduced mindfulness practice for stress and anxiety to the Western medical establishment. He reframed the Buddhist concepts using scientific terminology, added some meditation exercises and yoga stretches, and developed an intensive eight-to-ten-week mindfulness-based stress reduction (MBSR) program that included forty minutes of mindfulness meditation practice each day as homework. He recruited into the program a group of chronic-pain patients who weren't responding to regular medical treatment. Incredibly, these participants reported less pain, improved mood, and better mental health from the beginning to end of the mindfulness-based program (Kabat-Zinn 1982; Kabat-Zinn, Lipworth, and Burney 1985), and in comparison to a group of patients receiving the clinic's normal care (Kabat-Zinn, Lipworth, and Burney 1985). And thus the Mindful Revolution was born.

Today, mindfulness-based interventions for pain, stress, depression, anxiety, cancer, addiction, and chronic illness are accepted worldwide. The credibility of mindfulness exercises as an intervention for anxiety and stress and stress-related illness has been enhanced by its strong neuroscientific base. University of Wisconsin professor of psychology and psychiatry Richie Davidson has been instrumental in demonstrating how mindfulness works in the brain and how mindfulness for stress can change brain structure and functioning to facilitate stress resilience and mental health.

Dr. Davidson's research team used brain imaging technology to study mindfulness meditation techniques in Buddhist monks and novice meditators (Davidson et al. 2003; Lutz et al. 2004). Their findings suggest that "contemplative practices" such as meditation and mindfulness can improve compassion, empathy, kindness, and attention in the brain. These studies powerfully demonstrate neuroplasticity—that even adult brains can change their structure and pathways with repeated practice of new habits. By practicing mindfulness techniques for stress, you can learn to redirect the emotional reactivity of your stress response into more calm, peaceful, and attentive states.

Mindfulness and Your Amygdala

Your feelings of stress and anxiety result from your amygdala's seeing external experiences or even your own emotions as threats. This is a problem, both because it's impossible to escape many stressful experiences and because it's impossible to stop stress-related emotions from arising.

The location of your amygdala—in the middle of your brain, beneath your cortex—means that it receives information about threats and initiates your stress response very rapidly, sometimes even before the thinking parts of your brain know what's happening. In other words, you can't stop your amygdala from trying to protect you by initiating a stress response when it senses a change in circumstances that could lead to danger, loss, or pain. And you probably wouldn't want it to! Without your amygdala, you might waltz into traffic, stick your hand on a hot stove, or hang out with unsavory characters without realizing the danger. But you do need to manage your amygdala so that it doesn't compound your stress and anxiety or create unnecessary suffering for you. Using mindfulness techniques for stress and anxiety allows your prefrontal cortex to calm your amygdala when it overreacts, so you can avoid the Buddha's second arrow (unnecessary suffering), resulting in stress reduction.

Mindfulness skills are the antidote to the amygdala's rapid reactivity. With mindfulness techniques for anxiety and stress, you can learn to slow things down long enough for the prefrontal cortex to get on board and steer you through the stressful rough waters. Mindfulness meditation practice also creates a calm, relaxed state of mind that prompts your parasympathetic nervous system to calm down the physiology of the "fight, flight, or freeze" response and return to balance. Mindful states of mind send signals to your body that slow down your breathing and your heart rate. They tell your parasympathetic nervous system that the danger has passed and it can bring the body back to balance. In the next section, you'll learn more about what mindfulness for stress and anxiety is and how you can practice mindfulness-based stress reduction to calm down your amygdala.

What Is Mindfulness?

Think of mindfulness for stress and anxiety as both an attitude toward living and a resilient brain skill that reduces your amygdala's reactivity. Jon Kabat-Zinn defined mindfulness practice as a way of paying attention purposefully and with nonjudgmental acceptance to your present-moment experience (1994). When you practice adopting the stance of mindfulness for anxiety and stress toward your own experience in the moment, whatever that may be, you open up the space to sit peacefully with and examine your thoughts, feelings, or body sensations, rather than following your amygdala's instructions to run away, be overwhelmed, or react impulsively. You replace fear of your own inner experience with a curious, gentle, welcoming attitude—free of judgment, self-blame, and aversion. Mindfulness techniques for anxiety and stress reduction allow you to remain grounded in the present moment even when you face difficult stressors, so that your stressful feelings and anxiety feel more manageable or less overwhelming.

Mindfulness for stress and anxiety is a state of mind, a deliberate, purposeful, focused way of looking at your experience in the present. Rather than experiencing stress or anxiety on automatic pilot, when you're mindful, you look at your feelings of stress and anxiety from an observer vantage point. With mindfulness practice, you're aware of the stress and anxiety flowing through your mind and body without feeling totally merged with it. You maintain the awareness that stress is a moving, dynamic state that's flowing through you but that it isn't all that you are. You're more than whatever's happening in your mind and body at the moment. Mindfulness meditation teachers often use the metaphor that you are the sky and your thoughts and feelings are clouds. The clouds float by, but the sky is always there. The sky provides the canvas for the clouds to float on. So you're the sky, and your feelings of stress and anxiety are the clouds. You can sit out the storm until the sky is clear!

The most common anchor used in teaching mindfulness techniques for stress and anxiety is your breath. When you get stressed or anxious, your breathing becomes faster and more shallow as your sympathetic nervous system readies your body for fighting or fleeing. When the stressful situation is over, your parasympathetic nervous system begins slowing your breath and heart rate to put the brakes on your stress response. With mindfulness exercises for anxiety and stress, you deliberately focus on your breath in a way that slows it down, even though this isn't the explicit goal—the goal is just to watch your breath. With mindfulness for anxiety and stress reduction, your breathing becomes slower and more rhythmic, which slows down your heart rate. The parts of your brain responsible for sensing movement and breathing send signals to your amygdala that the threat is over, and the whole system begins to calm down.

The best way to understand how your body reacts to mindfulness for stress and anxiety is to experience mindfulness-based stress reduction. The following mindfulness meditation technique will teach you to focus on your breath in a mindful way. The more often you do these sorts of mindfulness exercises for anxiety and stress, the more quickly you'll develop an attitude of mindfulness.

Exercise: A Simple Breath Awareness Meditation

Here are some instructions for a basic breath awareness mindfulness meditation. Do this once or twice a day for two weeks, and observe what happens. There's no right or wrong way to do this mindfulness practice for stress and anxiety. Try to accept whatever your individual experience is. The goal is not to achieve perfect focus on your breath, but rather to learn how your mind works! It's normal for your mind to wander, but when you catch your mind wandering and deliberately bring it back, you're learning to mindfully control the focus of your attention.

1. Pick a comfortable, quiet place where you won't be disturbed.

2. Sit with your spine upright on a cushion on the floor or a chair. If you use a chair, make sure your feet are touching the ground. Close your eyes, or maintain a soft, unfocused gaze.

3. Begin to notice your breathing. Try to maintain an open and curious attitude. Notice where your breath goes when it enters and leaves your body.

4. Don't try to force or change your breath in any way. It may change naturally as you observe it.

5. If your mind wanders, note what it's doing, and then gently bring your attention back to your breath.

6. Continue observing your breath for eight to ten minutes. At the end of the practice, notice how your mind and body feel, then slowly come back to the room.

As you continue this mindfulness practice for stress reduction for two weeks, notice if your mind resists the idea of change by creating judgmental thoughts such as I won't be able to keep it up or It won't do any good. You don't have to believe your judgmental thoughts; just notice them. Try to replace your judgmental attitude with one of curiosity, and keep an open mind so that you don't prematurely limit your experience.

In addition to paying attention in an open,

nonjudgmental way, there are other characteristics of a mindful state of mind that create a powerful shift in brain functioning. In the next section, we'll discuss them in detail.

Characteristics of a Mindful State of Mind

Being mindful is more than meditating or focusing on your breath. Rather, it's a state of mind, characterized by the following attributes.

1. An Observing Stance

Mindfulness for anxiety and stress doesn't take away your stressful thoughts and feelings, but it changes your relationship to them. It's as if you're an observer who can look at these feelings without getting consumed by them or pushing them away. Thus, being mindful gives you more mental space and freedom. You don't have to be controlled by your stress response; you can redirect your focus, thereby gaining more control over your behavior when stressed.

2. Slowing Things Down

When your amygdala senses a stressor, it acts very quickly to "hijack" your brain for emergency action. However, not every stressor is an emergency, and successfully dealing with most stressors requires thinking of solutions, tolerating anxiety and uncertainty, and adapting to new situations. These are all functions of your prefrontal cortex, which is slower to receive and process information than your amygdala. Therefore, the first step in being mindful is to slow things down so that you can take a broader view of the situation before reacting.

Mindfulness for stress and anxiety moves your mind out of "acting" mode into "watching" mode, taking away the sense of urgency and giving your mind and body time to get back in sync.

3. Focusing on the Present Moment

When you practice mindfulness for anxiety and stress, you focus your attention deliberately and openly on what's happening in the present moment, both within you and around you. You may notice and describe your sensory experience—what you're seeing, hearing, feeling, or smelling right at that moment. Or you may focus on your breath to see what's happening inside and to ground yourself. This awareness of the present helps you stop ruminating about the past or worrying about the future.

4. Replacing Fear with Curiosity

Mindfulness for anxiety and stress replaces fear and emotional reactivity with an open, spacious curiosity. What's that thought or feeling that's arising? What does it look like and feel like? Is this something helpful or important that you want to focus on, or is it just an automatic event that you can observe as it passes through you? How does this emotion or experience change and unfold over time?

5. Openness and Non-judgment

Non-judgment is a key part of a mindfulness practice for stress and anxiety. When your amygdala triggers your stress response, you automatically begin to label the situation or your reactions as a threat that you need to escape. This is the aversion that the Buddha referred to as the second arrow. By observing your judging mind— a key mindfulness technique—you can avoid automatically buying into these negative judgments. You can then deliberately redirect your mind back to observing your thoughts and feelings with an open mind. This transforms your experience of stress by taking the terror and panic out of it.

6. An Attitude of Equanimity

Based on the Buddha's original teachings about non-attachment to pleasure or pain, a mindfulness attitude is one of peace, balance, and equanimity. To have equanimity means to let go of "needing" things to be a certain way. Equanimity keeps us from getting shot by that second arrow of addictive cravings or feelings of panic and desperation.

Everything is impermanent, everything is changing, and many important life outcomes are at least partially out of our control. Therefore, we need to stand firm and not be swept off balance by stress and anxiety.

7. "Being" Instead of "Doing"

When you're stressed, your amygdala creates an

impetus for action to eliminate the threat so that you can be safe. Finding solutions or learning new skills in a stressful situation requires a goal-oriented mind-set. But your mind and body also need periods of rest and quiet so that you don't get depleted by too much "doing." Mindfulness for stress and anxiety teaches you how to just "be" in the moment, without any particular goal or outcome and without judging your experience or wanting to be rid of it.

In the next section, you'll learn to deliberately focus on your body or your sensory experience with mindful openness and curiosity.

The "How" of Mindfulness

It sometimes takes weeks or even months of practice to really understand what it means to be mindful. Following are different ways of practicing mindfulness for stress and anxiety. Try all of them, or find the one that works best for you. Research shows that practicing mindfulness for at least thirty minutes per day can actually shrink your amygdala (Hölzel et al. 2011).

Optimize your environment for practicing

mindfulness for anxiety and stress. You may want to create a "meditation corner" with a comfortable pillow and some pleasant objects for you to focus on. A scented candle, a flower, or a smooth stone can be an anchor for your mindful attention, as I'll describe later in the book. Set aside a time every day for mindfulness practice, and put it in your schedule. You can practice mindfulness for stress and anxiety lying in bed, sitting cross-legged or in a chair, or even while walking, as you'll see below. Find the way that works for you. You don't always have to practice for thirty minutes. Studies show that five to twenty minutes of meditation per day for five weeks creates some of the same brain changes as longer periods of meditation (Moyer et al. 2011) I suggest you start with eight to ten minutes a day of formal practice and then gradually increase the length of your mindfulness meditations.

And so your mindfulness journey for stress reduction begins.

Exercise: Mindfulness of Your Breath

This mindfulness practice is the one I use most

frequently with my clients because it allows you to really feel and connect with your breath and also to feel grounded and solid in your body. It's my adaptation (with permission) of a mindfulness practice used by Daniel Siegel, author of many books and courses on mindfulness and the brain. This version of the instructions is for when you sit upright on the couch. Feel free to adapt the wording if you're lying on the floor or bed.

1. Sit comfortably on the couch with an upright yet relaxed pose.

Now close your eyes or maintain a soft gaze. Let your mind and body begin to settle into the practice, noticing what your body feels like.

2. Focus your attention on your feet. Notice all the parts of your feet that are touching the floor. Notice your toes; where your toes join your foot; the middle of your foot; your heel; your ankle; the whole bottom of your foot; the inside and the outside.

3. Let your feet sink into the floor, noticing the support of the earth and feeling it ground you.

4. Begin to notice all the parts of your body that touch the couch— the back of your thighs, your seat, perhaps your back, your arms, and your hands. Let your hands and feet sink into the support of the couch and floor. Notice how your body feels as you sit, supported by the couch and floor.

5. Begin to notice your breath. Just breathe easily for a few breaths, noticing where your breath goes as you breathe in and as you breathe out. Notice the pause between your in-breath and your out-breath. If your mind wanders—as it probably will, because that's what minds do— just notice where it goes for an instant and then slowly, gently, direct your attention back to your breath.

Continue to do this as you begin to notice your breath in your nose, chest, and belly.

6. Slowly, bring your attention to your breath as it enters your nostrils. Notice whether it's hot or cold, light or heavy, and slow or fast. How does it feel? Notice where your breath touches your nostrils as you breathe in and as you breathe out.

Continue to notice your breath in your nostrils for a few minutes.

7. Begin to notice your breath in your chest. Notice how your chest moves up and down with your breath like a wave, moving up as you breathe in and down as you breathe out. Just notice your chest as it expands and contracts with your breath. Watch the rhythmic wave in your chest as you breathe in and as you breathe out.

Continue watching your chest for a few minutes.

8. Direct your attention downward, toward your belly. You can put your hand on your belly to help you connect with the spot just below your belly button. This spot is at the very core and center of your body. Notice how your belly moves out when you breathe in and how it moves in when you breathe out. There's no need to force or change your breath in any way. And if your mind wanders, bring it back to your belly kindly and gently. As you notice your breath in your belly, notice whether your breath changes or stays the same. Notice the rhythm of your breath in your belly.

9. As you notice your breath in your belly, begin to expand your attention outward toward your whole body. Begin to notice your whole body breathing as a single unit—breathing in and breathing out in a slow, steady rhythm. Notice the waves of breath as they move in and out of your body—filling your nose, the back of your throat, your chest, your ribcage, your belly, and your whole body with fresh, cleansing air. Notice how your breath travels through your body, and see whether it seems to open up any space in the area it touches. Just notice the rhythm of your whole body breathing as one: first the in-breath, then the pause between the breaths, and finally the out-breath. Breathing in and breathing out...

10. Slowly, begin to bring your attention back to the couch, to your hands and feet. Slowly open your eyes and begin to notice the room around you. Take your time, and notice how your body feels now. Is there any difference from when you began the mindfulness practice?

When my clients do this mindfulness practice, many report a deep sense of peace, comfort, and calm. Feeling stressed can create tension, tightness, and constriction in your body, particularly in your chest and belly. This mindfulness-based stress-reduction practice can help open up space in these areas. A mindful focus creates distance from feelings of stress and generates a sense of peace and well-being.

Your breath is a powerful anchor for your attention, but this isn't the only way to practice mindfulness for anxiety and stress. You can also use your senses to create a sense of present-moment awareness and inner peace, as you'll see in the next mindfulness practice.

Exercise: Mindfulness of Your Senses

When your amygdala sounds the alarm bells, you lose touch with the present moment as your emergency response kicks in. You may feel compelled to "do something" about the stressor or to run away from the overwhelming feelings. By deliberately focusing attention on your senses instead, you move from a "doing," "getting," or "avoiding" mindset to "noticing and describing" what's around you. This mindfulness technique for stress reduction helps you feel more present and connected. We connect with the outside world through our senses. When we're mindful of what's around us, we gain awareness that we're part of a larger world of living and inanimate objects. Connecting with your senses can also be a way of what psychologist Rick Hanson (2009) calls taking in the good, or deliberately directing your brain to focus on relaxing or pleasant things in a way that helps calm down your stress response.

Walking in nature is a wonderful way to practice mindfulness of the senses. Being outdoors and close to nature has a calming influence on your brain and body, a natural backdrop for mindfulness meditation for anxiety. When you can't get outside, you can still practice mindfulness of your senses by adjusting the following practice to your situation. You can sit on your deck or in your garden or even look out the window, or you can look at pictures or photographs of nature scenes.

Exciting new research shows that walking outside in green spaces or even looking at nature scenes can increase your mind and body's resilience to stress. A study of college students (Bratman et al. 2015) showed that walking in green campus parkland reduced anxiety and worry more than walking in a busy street and had some cognitive benefits as well. In another study (Van den Berg et al. 2015), students were shown one of two types of pictures: either nature scenes, with trees and empty pathways, or urban scenes, with cars and people. They were then given a stressful math test. Those who had been shown pictures of trees had faster cardiovascular recovery (for example, their heart rate returned to normal more quickly after the test was over) than those who had viewed urban scenes. Measures of vagal tone showed that their parasympathetic nervous systems were better able to put the brakes on their "fight or flight" response. Benefits of mindfulness for stress reduction can occur whether the scene is one or three dimensional.

Mindfulness of Your Senses in Nature

As you walk or sit in nature, begin to notice your surroundings as a whole, noticing also how you feel in these surroundings. Notice that you're not alone—you're a part of the rhythm and pace of nature.

1. Bring your attention slowly to what you see. Notice the colors: the rich browns of the earth, the greens of the trees, or the blues of the sky or water. Are the colors bright or muted? Notice which ones draw your attention. Notice light and shadows, shapes and textures. Which surfaces are smooth, and which are uneven? Which are shiny, and which are dull? Which have sharp angles, and which are rounded? Just notice everything that you see. Now pay particular attention to one object—perhaps a tree or a flower— and notice its color, shape, and texture.

2. Focus on what you hear. Perhaps you hear the chirping of birds, the sound of the wind, or a babbling brook. Notice the sounds your feet make as they crunch on the gravel or sink into the earth. Do you hear people's voices? Do you hear a dog barking? Notice the pitch and rhythm of the sounds. Which ones draw you in? Notice how the sounds emerge and then fade away—try to notice the silence between the sounds. Now pick one of these sounds to focus on. Notice its

tone, pitch, and rhythm. Notice whether it stays the same or changes.

3. Notice what you smell. The smells around you may be sweet or spicy, earthy or fresh, faint or intense. Now pick just one smell to focus on—perhaps the breeze, the earth, or the flowers—and notice everything you can about it.

4. Notice what you feel. Notice the temperature of the air. Notice the feeling of the sun or the fresh breeze on your skin. Notice whether the air is moving fast or slow. Notice the feeling of the ground beneath your feet.

5. Notice how you feel inside your body. What's it like inside your chest, your back, and your belly? Do you feel any more spacious and calm than when you began this practice? Do you feel any part of you letting go of tension?

6. Notice how your feet feel as you walk. Try to slow the pace of your walking so that you notice each step: Right foot up, moving forward, and then down. Left foot up, moving forward, and then down…

For a short version of this mindfulness practice for stress reduction, pay attention to just one sense.

For example, focus only on what you see, hear, smell, or feel. Or just notice each step you take as you walk, without focusing on your surroundings. You can also do this mindfulness practice for stress and anxiety just about anywhere, at any time—not just in nature.

Exercise: Mindfulness of Objects

Another mindfulness exercise to calm your stressed-out brain is to focus on what's around you. If you're feeling stressed or anxious while making a presentation, interviewing for a job, taking an exam, or getting ready for an important dinner party, try silently naming three objects in the room and describing their color, shape, and texture as a quick and easy way of moving your mind from "fight, flight, or freeze" mode to "notice and describe" mode.

At home, create a "mindfulness corner" where you keep objects with interesting colors, textures, smells, or sounds. Use it as a sanctuary when you feel stressed, or simply practice your mindfulness exercises for anxiety and stress reduction there daily.

Each time you visit your "mindfulness corner," spend a few minutes examining the sensory qualities of each object. Look at it, touch it, smell it, and taste it if appropriate. Things that might work well for this purpose include seashells, smooth stones, scented candles, mints, sprigs of lavender or rosemary, flowers or leaves, lemons, small glass bottles, wooden beads, soft fabric, and hand cream. You can also buy traditional meditation objects such as a mindfulness bell, a Tibetan singing bowl, a small statue of the Buddha, or a Himalayan salt candle.

The options are limited only by your budget!

The exercises in this book are great ways to learn and practice mindfulness for anxiety and stress. Yet, as we discussed earlier, mindfulness is also a state of mind and a way of living that's larger than any particular practice.

Practicing mindfulness teaches you a stress-proof attitude that you can integrate into every aspect of your daily life. And the more you integrate mindfulness or stress and anxiety into your life, the more opportunity you'll have to calm your amygdala when it starts trying to hijack your brain. In the following section, you'll learn some ways of making mindfulness part of your daily routine.

Integrating Mindfulness into Your Everyday Life

When you're feeling stressed or anxious, it's often because you have too much to do and too little time or because you're dealing with an emotionally difficult situation. Stress takes your mind away from the present moment as your amygdala focuses your attention on what will happen if you don't solve the problems or complete the tasks. Your mind may get tired and murky; you may find yourself getting distracted or zoning out instead of focusing on what's most important. You may run around on automatic pilot as your heart races and your breathing shortens in "fight, flight, or freeze" mode. These triggers serve to remind you to choose mindfulness to deal with stress and anxiety.

The following practice is adapted from a practice used by Dr. Elisha Goldstein (Goldstein 2010). Use it to become more mindful from the moment you wake up until you go to bed at night, constantly redirecting your brain back to the present and weakening your amygdala's power to take away your sense of peace and connection with the world.

Integrating Mindfulness into Your Daily Routine

When you first wake up, instead of jumping out of bed, make time for the STOP practice described here. It'll help you start your day off on a mindful note. Continue to use this mindfulness practice throughout the day whenever you begin to feel stressed or anxious, as a way of grounding yourself when stress begins to creep in.

1. Stop. Stop whatever you're doing, and bring your mind back to the present moment.

2. Take a breath. Take a few deep breaths to slow down your "fight, flight, or freeze" response.

3. Observe. Begin to notice what you're feeling, thinking, and doing.

What's going on in your body? Describe any bodily sensations (such as tightness in your throat or shoulders) you become aware of. Is there an emotion word you can use to describe these feelings (such as "angry" or "scared")? Try to stay in the moment with these feelings and "breathe into them": imagine sending your breath into the areas that feel tight, constricted, or activated by these feelings.

4. Proceed. When you're feeling sufficiently present and aware, go about your business in a deliberate way. You may want to simply continue what you were doing, but with a more mindful demeanor.

Here are some other ways to integrate mindfulness for anxiety and stress into your life as you get ready for and go about your day:

When you observe your morning routine, notice if your mind is already at work or school, worrying or planning how to deal with your daily tasks and challenges. When you notice your amygdala hijacking your thoughts, bring your attention back to the present moment. If you're in the shower, notice the flow, temperature, and sound of the water, the bubbles, and the smell of the soap. When you drink your morning coffee, notice the smell of the coffee beans, the warmth of the cup, and the taste of the first sip. As you eat your breakfast, slow down and pay attention to the sight, smell, and taste of the food and how it feels to chew and swallow. Mornings offer multiple opportunities to practice your mindfulness-based stress reduction skills.

Mindfully greet the other members of your household or your pets. Slow down and focus on what they're saying and their nonverbal expressions. Focus on your feelings of love for them.

Take time to say good-bye as you leave the house.

On your way to your destination, notice what your mind is doing. Try leaving the house a little earlier so that you can walk or drive more slowly. Let the things you would normally see as interruptions or obstacles (such as red lights or delays) be reminders to practice mindfulness for

DANIEL ANDERSON

anxiety and stress reduction. If you feel yourself getting angry or impatient with the traffic or long red lights, direct your attention to your breath or focus on the things you see around you—the cars, the people walking by, the trees, the sky, and so on.

As you walk into work or school, drop off your children, or go about your errands, check in with your body and notice any tension.

Bring yourself back to the present moment by slowing down and focusing on your breathing, what you see around you, or the feelings in your feet as you walk. Do the STOP practice if you begin to notice bodily tension or negative emotions arising

Practice STOP before checking your phone, checking your e-mail, or logging into social media. Set time limits for these tasks, and don't let them sway you into mindless reactivity that distracts you from what's most important.

Use STOP or breath awareness mindfulness practices throughout the day.

Notice if your muscles are tense, if your breathing is shallow, or if your mind is wandering. Notice if you're feeling reactive, spaced out, or focused and alert. Change your focus by moving or stretching for a few minutes, practicing mindful breathing, or getting some fresh air.

Mindfulness is a skill you learn through repeated practice. It represents a shift in perspective away from constant focus on stressors and amygdala-driven reactivity. It allows your mind and body to rest peacefully and enjoy the moment despite the stress. Stress can be there, but it doesn't have to consume you and take you away from the people you love, getting your work done, looking after your health, and being present in your life. But mindfulness for anxiety and stress is more than a change in attitude.

With a regular mindfulness practice for anxiety and stress reduction and by adopting a mindful attitude toward living, you can actually change the structure of your brain, as you'll see in the next section.

How Mindfulness Calms Down Your Amygdala

Researchers have been studying the effects of mindfulness on the brain and body for more than twenty-five years using sophisticated technologies such as functional magnetic resonance imaging (fMRI) to scan the brain in real time. They have measured effects of mindfulness on depression, anxiety, physiological responses, blood pressure, and resistance to illness. There's now a wide body of evidence showing that mindfulness meditation works to reduce your body and brain's response to stress, taking away some of your amygdala's power to steer you off course.

Mindfulness-based interventions are associated with improved mood, reduced anxiety, better coping when stressed, enhanced emotion regulation, and less physiological reactivity (such as sweating and rapid heartbeat) in response to stressors. A meta-analysis that pooled the results of twenty mindfulness studies concluded that "the consistent and relatively strong level of effect sizes across very different types of sample indicates that mindfulness training might enhance general features of coping with distress and disability in everyday life, as well as under more extraordinary conditions of serious disorder or stress" (Grossman et al. 2003, 39). This meta-analysis showed that mindfulness training reduced disability and improved mood and quality of life in people dealing with a variety of physical illnesses (such as cancer, chronic pain, and heart disease) and mental health issues. Mindfulness interventions have also been shown to reliably reduce anxiety, depression, and stress in healthy people (Chiesa and Serretti 2009; Khoury et al. 2013).

Studies show that mindfulness training for stress can make the amygdala less reactive to stressors. A study by researchers at the University Hospital Zurich (Lutz et al. 2014) focused on whether mindfulness training for anxiety and stress reduction could affect the brain when subjects viewed pictures designed to trigger emotions. One group of subjects was given mindfulness training, and the other group (the control group) wasn't. Then both groups were shown pictures while their brains were scanned. Subjects were given clues that indicated whether the next picture would be positive, negative, neutral, or unknown (meaning there was a fifty-fifty chance it could be positive or negative). The subjects in the mindfulness group were instructed to use their mindfulness skills (for example, noticing their reactions without judgment) when the clue indicated that an unpleasant or unknown picture was coming. The brain scans showed that, compared to the control group, subjects in the mindfulness group had less activity in the amygdala and in brain regions involved in negative emotion when they anticipated seeing negative or unknown pictures.

Repeated practice of mindfulness for anxiety and stress over weeks or months may even change the structure of your amygdala. In a study by Harvard Medical School researchers (Hölzel et al. 2011), an eight-week mindfulness course led not only to reduced stress and anxiety but also to changes in the brain: the amount of nerve cells and neural connections shrank in the amygdala but increased in the hippocampus. Neither of these brain changes was found in the control group.

Scientists have pooled data from more than twenty studies (Fox et al. 2014) to show that mindfulness for stress and anxiety reduction affects at least eight different brain areas associated with self-regulation, memory, focus, motivation, compassion, and resilience. In particular, mindfulness can strengthen your hippocampus, an area that has many cortisol receptors and can be damaged by chronic stress. Your hippocampus can help you mentally process and file away stressful memories so that they're less likely to be triggered later. This suggests that mindfulness practices can make your brain more resilient to stress.

These research results are exciting, because they prove that you don't have to live in a monastery or on a mountaintop to calm your amygdala and strengthen your hippocampus with mindfulness-based stress reduction techniques.

Practicing mindfulness for stress over time makes your amygdala less reactive to negative events or uncertainty in your environment and helps your hippocampus process stressful events more effectively. In this chapter, you learned about mindfulness for anxiety and stress as both a practice and an approach to living that can help you better deal with stress.

Mindfulness meditation has its roots in ancient Buddhist philosophy, but it has been adapted for Western use. Being mindful means having an open, accepting, and compassionate attitude toward your own experience in the present moment, whatever that may be. It means allowing, rather than pushing away your inner experience; it means being in the moment, rather than constantly worrying or rushing around.

Mindfulness-based interventions have helped reduce people's feelings of stress, lower their blood pressure, and improve their resistance to illness. Mental health professionals use such mindfulness interventions to treat depression, anxiety, and substance abuse. Mindfulness has also been shown to shrink the amygdala (the brain's alarm center) and protect the hippocampus from being damaged by stress. The mindfulness exercises in this chapter can help you reduce your reactivity to stress and anxiety.

CHAPTER SEVEN

RECOVERY GUIDE TO ANXIETY DISORDERS

Getting rid of anxiety disorders isn't the same as taking out the trash. If you take your trash out to the curb, it's gone forever, and won't come back. But when you try to dispose of chronic anxiety, you often find that this task is more like the child's game, "Whack a Mole", than it's like taking out the trash. Each time you hit a mole, more moles pop up. Every effort that you make to fight against anxiety, invites more of it.

So you need to be able to work smart, not hard, to overcome anxiety disorders. This guide will help you do that.

The Anxiety Trick

The fears, phobias, and worry that you experience with chronic anxiety disorders often seem "irrational", and difficult to overcome.

That's because there is a "Trick" to chronic anxiety problems. Have you ever wondered why fears and phobias seem like such difficult problems to solve? The reason is that chronic fears literally trick you into thinking and acting in ways that make the problem more chronic. You can't learn to float through anxiety disorders if you don't understand the Anxiety Trick.

The outcome of the Anxiety Trick is that people get fooled into trying to solve their anxiety problems with methods that can only make them worse. They get fooled into "putting out fires with gasoline".

The Key Fears of Anxiety Disorders

There are six principal anxiety disorders. The fears are different, but each one relies on the same Anxiety Trick, and draws upon the same kinds of anxiety symptoms.

And in each case, the person tries to extinguish the fears by responding in ways that actually make the problem worse and more chronic. Here are the key fears, and typical responses, of the six main anxiety disorders.

Panic Disorder and Agoraphobia

A person with Panic Disorder and Agoraphobia fears that a panic attack will disable him in some way - kill him, make him crazy, make him faint, and so on. In response, he often goes to great lengths to protect himself from a panic attack, by avoiding ordinary activities and locations; by carrying objects, like water bottles and cell phones, that he hopes will protect him; by trying to distract himself from the subject of panic; and numerous other strategies will ultimately make the problem more persistent and severe, rather than less.

The fear of driving is often a part of panic disorder.

If panic attacks and phobias are your principal anxiety concern, my Panic Attacks Workbook is a useful guide to recovery from these problems.

Social Anxiety Disorder (or Social Phobia)

A person with Social Phobia fears becoming so visibly and unreasonably afraid in front of other people that they will judge her as a weak, inadequate person, and no longer associate with her. In response, she often goes to great lengths to avoid social experiences, hoping that this avoidance will save her from embarrassment and public humiliation. However, her avoidance of social situations leads her to become more, rather than less, fearful of them, and also leads to social isolation.

The fear of public speaking, and the broader fear of stage fright are considered to be specific instances of Social Phobia.

Specific Phobia

A Specific Phobia is a pattern of excessive fear of some ordinary object, situation, or activity. A person with a fear of dogs, for instance, may fear that a dog will attack him; or he may be afraid that he will "lose his mind", or run into heavy traffic, on encountering a dog.

People with phobias usually try to avoid what they fear. Unfortunately, this often creates greater problems for them. Not only do they continue to fear the object, but the avoidance restricts their freedom to enjoy life as they would see fit.

A specific phobia is usually distinguished from Panic Disorder by its narrow focus. A person with a fear of flying who has no fear of other enclosed spaces would likely be considered to have a specific phobia. A person who fears airplanes, elevators, tunnels, and bridges is usually considered to have Panic Disorder or claustrophobia. However, the fear of public speaking is usually considered to be a part of Social Phobia.

A person with a Blood Phobia may fear a variety of situations, but they all involve the prospect of seeing blood. A person with a fear of vomiting (either fearing that they will vomit, or that that they'll see someone else vomit) would be considered to have Emetophobia. The official definitions of some of these disorders will change in 2013, so don't get preoccupied with the label.

Whether you have one or multiple phobias, these are very treatable conditions.

Obsessive Compulsive Disorder (OCD)

A person with Obsessive Compulsive Disorder experiences intrusive, unwelcome thoughts (called obsessions) which are so persistent and upsetting that he fears the thoughts might not stop.

In response, he tries to stop having those thoughts with a variety of efforts (called compulsions). Unfortunately, the compulsions usually become a severe, upsetting problem themselves.

For example, a man may have obsessive thoughts that he might pass swine flu on to his children, even though he doesn't have the flu himself, and wash his hands repetitively in an effort to get rid of that thought. Or a woman may have obsessive thoughts that she left the garage door open, and repeatedly check the garage all night in an effort to stop thinking that. Not only do these efforts fail to rid the person of the unwelcome thoughts, they become a new form of torment in that person's life.

Generalized Anxiety Disorder

A person with Generalized Anxiety Disorder worries repeatedly and continually about a wide variety of possible problems, and becomes so consumed by worry that she fears the worry will eventually kill her or drive her to a "nervous breakdown". In response, she often tries a wide variety of "thought control" methods she hopes will enable her to "stop thinking about it." Distraction is one such effort. Unfortunately, the effort to stop thinking about it actually makes the worrisome thoughts more persistent.

If persistent worry is a big part of your anxiety concerns, The Worry Trick is a useful guide to reducing the disruptive role worry plays in your life.

Post-Traumatic Stress Disorder (PTSD)

A person who has witnessed or experienced some dangerous or life threatening event (a shooting or a car crash) fears that the subsequent thoughts and powerful reminders of that event will lead to a loss of control or mental illness. The powerful symptoms of fear and upset a person experiences when recalling a terrible event are reactions to that event. However, the person gets tricked into responding to these reactions as if they were warnings of an upcoming danger, rather than reminders of a past one.

And Depression, too?

It's very common for people to experience depression in response to the way anxiety disorders have disrupted their lives. Less frequently, sometimes people experienced a strong depression before the anxiety set in, and this is a different kind of problem. Either way, depressive symptoms need to be addressed in recovery, so it's useful t

Exposure Therapy for Fears and Phobias

Exposure Therapy has been shown to be the most effective anxiety treatment for people with many anxiety disorders. You might already know that it involves practicing with what you fear, in order to become less afraid. But how does it work?

Exposure Therapy helps you retrain your brain. It's not just about "getting used to" the fear. It's about retraining your brain to stop sending the fear signal when there isn't any danger.

People struggle against anxiety attacks and

phobias because they recognize that their fears are exaggerated and illogical. They try hard to talk themselves out of the fear.

But that doesn't help. So they end up trying to avoid the fear, and that, unfortunately, just strengthens it.

Exposure Therapy will help you retrain your brain to let go of phobias, anxiety attacks, and other forms of anxiety disorders.

Let's see how Exposure Therapy works.

Fight or Flight

When your brain gets a signal of danger, it triggers an immediate response, the familiar Fight or Flight response. That's a good thing, because when we face danger, we need to react quickly and powerfully.

Humans evolved in a different world than the one we inhabit today. It was a world full of predators, without police or deadbolt locks. Our main job was to get enough to eat each day without becoming food for somebody else. We needed a good emergency alert system to keep us out of the jaws of predators.

If we had relied on the thinking, intellectual part of our brain, called the cerebral cortex, to keep us safe, we'd be extinct. It's too slow. It's good for writing a speech, and figuring out your income tax, but not for making snap decisions about danger.

The part of your brain that handles these Fight or Flight responses is very different from the part of the brain you're most familiar with.

The Amygdala

The Amygdala, a little almond shaped part of your brain, is what makes these Fight or Flight decisions. The Amygdala works quickly, without your conscious awareness, because speed is vital in protecting against threats. You only find out what the Amydgala did when you feel its effects in your body (all the familiar panic sensations) and in your behavior (duck, run, escape).

Whenever we make a decision, there are two possible kinds of errors. One is a false positive. If you decide there's a tiger hiding in the tall grass, when there isn't one, that's a false positive. When you make a false positive error, you get afraid in the absence of danger, but you don't get eaten.

The second type is a false negative. If you decide there's no tiger hiding in the tall grass when there really is one, that's a false negative. When you make this false negative error, you feel okay, but you're gonna get eaten.

Your Amygdala doesn't care how many times it scares you unnecessarily. It just aims to keep you alive. It doesn't want to make any false negative mistakes.

If you experience phobias and anxiety attacks, and want to overcome them, you need a form of anxiety treatment which will retrain this part of your brain. The most direct and systematic way to do that is Exposure Therapy.

How Your Amygdala Works

Your Amygdala is always watching, passively, in the background, for some sign of danger. When it sees one, true or false, it presses the "fight or flight" button and fills you with fear. When the danger is real, that's a good thing. But your Amygdala works like it's still 27,000 B.C., and will often make the mistake of seeing danger when there's none.

It Learns by Association, not Reason or Logic

When you run away from whatever the apparent danger is, the Amygdala stands down and goes back to quietly watching. If you ran away from a mugger, that's a good thing. But if you ran away from a grocery store, or a dog on a leash, that's a bad thing. Now your Amygdala will be conditioned to see the grocery store or the dog as dangerous, and will make you afraid next time you see one.

The Amygdala learns by association. It associates the crowded store, or the dog, with danger. It doesn't learn by conscious thought. This is why you can't simply talk yourself out of a phobia or anxiety attack. The fear memory is stored as a conditioned fear, and can only be relieved by more conditioning, not discussion or reason.

It only Learns When You're Afraid

The Amygdala only learns when it's fully activated, when it spots something it considers dangerous. It only forms new memories and associations, new lessons, when you've become afraid. The rest of the time it's on autopilot, passively watching.

Do you see what this means? If you stay away from what you fear, your Amygdala will keep on "believing" the same old mistakes, without a chance to learn anything new.

How Can You "Talk" to Your Amygdala?

Your Amygdala only learns from experience. If you flee the scene every time you have an anxiety attack, your Amygdala learns that you should leave to be safe.

How can you get your Amygdala to learn something new? You have to activate it by exposing yourself to a trigger that gets you afraid. If you have a dog phobia, that would be a dog. If you have anxiety attacks on subways (or highways), you need a subway (or a highway).

And you need to stay there with that fear until it gets a lot lower.

That gives your Amygdala the chance to learn that it got all worked up about nothing. That way, it can learn that dogs (or highways) aren't the threat that it had been conditioned to believe. And, with repetition, it will develop a new memory, one that lets you get on with your life without being disrupted by phobias and anxiety attacks.

Retraining Your Amygdala

That's how Exposure Therapy works. Exposure Therapy retrains your Amygdala.

You don't have to do this radically and quickly. What you need to do is to continually arrange to activate your Amygdala by exposing yourself to what you fear, and then stay in place, making sure that the fear leaves before you do. You can use a variety of coping steps to help you do that, or you can just "float", as Claire Weekes called it, and wait for the fear to subside. Either way, Exposure Therapy will enable you to retrain your Amygdala with new learning in ways it can absorb.

List of Tips

Tip One: Panic attacks: 13 tips to stop anxiety in its tracks

One in 10 people are believed to suffer from occasional panic attacks, often triggered by stressful events, while two in 100 UK people have panic disorder (recurring and regular panic attacks).

A panic attack is an episode of intense subjective fear, usually accompanied by symptoms such as trembling, sweating, heart palpitations and hyperventilating. So what can you do if you feel your panic rising?

Stand up tall

As soon as you feel a panic attack coming on, straighten your spine and stand or sit up straight. 'Not only does this trick you into feeling more powerful and in control, but it will also give you physically more space to breathe,' says Niels Eek , psychologist at personal development and mental wellbeing app Remente.

Get moving

Panic attacks can make our entire body seize up, responding to our perceived threat of danger. 'The best and most counter-intuitive thing to do is to start moving around,'. 'Do some stretches, go out for a walk, or simply walk around slowly.' Moving and exercise are found to instantly counter the effects of panic by reducing cortisol levels as well as lowering the risk of anxiety in the future.

Fiddle and fidget!

If movement isn't an option, for example if you are on a plane during take-off, try to distract yourself with a stress ball, some beads or even gum. 'Researchers at Tokyo Medical and Dental University found that repetitive and tactile motions distract the mind from the immediate feelings of panic' .

Splash yourself with water

Researchers in Japan found that cold water stimulates the parasympathetic system, which in turn slows down our heart rate, providing a calming effect. 'While you might finding the task of drinking water while you are panicking physically impossible, try splashing some on your face,' suggests Niels Eek.

Chew gum

A mental health study found that chewing gum for 14 days may improve levels of anxiety and mood. Chewing is known to reduce levels of the stress hormone cortisol found in the saliva. Fast chewing has been shown to have a more anxiety-busting effect than slow chewing.

Boost your magnesium

A study in the journal Neuropharmacology, found that low magnesium can make you anxious. 'Magnesium is the most important mineral for 'relaxing' nerves and muscles and is essential for the normal functioning of the nervous system, so is effective for panic attacks,' says nutritionist Shona Wilkinson.

Name your feelings one by one

Whenever you are in the middle of a panic attack, your brain struggles to focus on anything that isn't the immediate panic. 'However, if you start naming each feeling you experience, such as 'it's difficult to breathe' or 'I want to cry when this happens', it can help re-focus your brain and move away from the panic.

Try colouring in

Research has shown that focusing on a calming activity such as colouring in mandalas can help people with anxiety. It works by calming down the amygdala, the part of the brain that controls our fight or flight response and keeps some people in a state of worry, panic and hypervigilance, so if you feel the panic start to rise, start colouring. Findings from the study suggest that colouring in a reasonably complex geometric pattern may induce a calming meditative state.

Go herbal

Herbal remedies have proven to be beneficial in halting panic attacks. 'Herbs which may be helpful in reducing anxiety include Valerian, Passionflower and St John's Wort,' says nutritionist Shona Wilkinson. 'These herbs may be a non-drug way to help reduce anxiety and help bring about a more calm state of being.'

Carry medication with you

'Some people find that carrying some beta-blocker tablets with them can be helpful (these are non-addictive tablets which could be prescribed by a GP or psychiatrist), and they work to switch off the bodily feelings of anxiety, such as heart palpitations and tremors,' says Psychiatrist Dr Ian Drever. 'Often just by having these tablets with them, it's reassuring enough to stop many people having a panic attack in the first place.'

Remember panic passes

Dr Drever urges you to remember that no matter how bad a panic attack feels, it can never hurt you. 'It may feel like you're going to stop breathing, suffocate or have a heart attack, but these are all features of a rush of adrenaline, and they will fade away with time, leaving no lasting trace. Panic always passes.'

Create a soothing playlist

Listening to music can help to reduce stress levels and quash anxiety. Classical music is particularly effective at slowing pulse and heart rate, lower blood pressure and decreasing levels of stress hormones. But it doesn't have to be classical – some people find that creating a playlist of music around 60-80bpm can be a really effective panic-buster.

'This makes intuitive sense as this is the speed of a resting heartbeat. It also helps to provide an external focus rather than on an excessive internal focus on what the body is doing in the heat of an anxious moment,' says Dr Drever.

Bring on your panic symptoms

The majority of panic attacks are accompanied by physical symptoms, such as an increased heart rate, inability to breathe, dizziness and others. 'Focusing on the symptoms and letting them take over can often make you feel worse,' says Eek. 'Instead, try inducing the symptoms on their own, outside of the panic attack – you will find that you have no fear of them and that your mind will eventually get bored and move onto other things.'

These tips are something you can definitely try, but if you're having serious panic attacks then it's important to see a GP and/or a CBT-psychologist. Treatments for panic attacks are really efficient, and if the above tips aren't enough, can provide a real, working solution.

Tip Two: Quick ways to calm your nerves

It is tough to control psychological strain; stress is a natural response to tricky situations and the outside world. Some circumstances are simply beyond our control, making coping hard to do. Fortunately, you do have control over how you react to situations. Learning healthy responses to stressors is a great place to start. As compiled from calmclinic.com, Oprah, Prevention and Women's Health magazine, here's how you can regain your cool even quicker than you lost it.

Chew a stick of gum

Researchers from Australia and England found that in moments of stress and anxiety, gum chewers felt less anxious and had 18 per cent less of the stress hormone cortisol in their saliva. "Chewing increases blood flow to the brain, which may make us feel more alert, and it may also distract us from stressors," says study co-author Dr Andrew Scholey, director of the Centre for Human Psychopharmacology at Swinburne University. The study suggests that chewing gum can de-stress you in as little as 10 minutes.

Brew black tea

The study of black tea —instead of green or herbal varieties — found it helps cut levels of the stress hormone cortisol circulating in the blood stream. People who drank four servings of black tea a day for six weeks were able to de-stress faster and had lower levels of cortisol after a stressful event, according to a study from University College London. Chemical compounds in the antioxidant-packed beverage may relax us through their effect on neurotransmitters in the brain.

Try a tennis ball massage

The International Journal of Neuroscience reported that a 15-minute self massage twice weekly can lower stress by soothing the sympathetic nervous system. It is an effective alternative, as compared to popping beta blockers and anti-anxiety meds. "Simply rolling a tennis ball over tense muscles like the spine, thighs and foot with the palm of your hand can trigger a calming response," says Dr Tiffany Field, director of Touch Research Institute at the University of Miami, School of Medicine.

Put pen to paper

A 2010 study in Anxiety, Stress & Coping found that writing about a stressful event for just 20 minutes on two different days lowered levels of perceived stress. Putting feelings on paper appears to organise thoughts and helps process unpleasant experiences and release negative emotions. This is a good way to confront your emotions, especially if you're naturally inclined to write. If things become jumbled, just keep writing. It's the process of thinking and recording your conflicts that is most important.

Tune in to music

"The body's internal rhythms entrain to the

external rhythms of music, like when you go to the sea, and you start breathing slower and your heart rate slows down and starts moving closer to the rhythm and pace of the ocean. It's the same with music," says Dr Frank Lipman, founder and director of Eleven-Eleven Wellness Centre. A study in the Journal of Advanced Nursing found that patients who listened to songs of their choice were less anxious and stressed. Boost your mood with clocking in at least 15 minutes of tune time daily.

Take a tech break

Before technology and smartphones, when you left your home or place of work, you most likely turned off the thoughts and emails related to it, too. Research shows we need mental breaks to refresh our minds and shut off the continuous stressors of work or classes. In a study by University of California, Irvine, and US Army researchers, heart rate monitors showed that checking e-mails and attending work calls put subjects on constant high alert with heart rates that indicated stress. "We found that shutting off e-mail eases anxiety," says study co-author Dr

Gloria Mark. Commit to no e-mail or social media activity for 45 minutes a day to begin weaning yourself off.

Start Counting Everything

The next time you feel panic setting in, start counting your sensations. As Anna Borges suggested on BuzzFeed, "Count five things you can see, four you can touch, three you can hear, two you can smell, and one you can taste." This is another distraction technique that requires you to focus in on things that are real — like the sounds in the room, or the feeling of your shirt against your skin — instead of just the panic in your mind. It's also a good trick to use when you're cooped up on a plane, or stuck some place where skipping around and dancing might attract undue attention.

Clean the house

Housework's repetitive nature can help release tension and calm anxious nerves. "We get lost in the rhythm of folding clothes, mopping or vacuuming, which can disrupt stressful thought patterns and trigger the body's relaxation response," says Dr Herbert Benson, director emeritus of the Benson-Henry Institute for Mind Body Medicine at Massachusetts General Hospital. Studies have found that cleaning carries emotional benefits — catharsis, clarity, control and change. These good feelings lead directly to self-improvement and empowerment. Who thought doing the dishes could have benefits!

Just Kick Back & Accept It

Sometimes none of the above techniques work and you find yourself fruitlessly naming feelings, or pawing at a wad of Silly Putty. When that happens, all you can do is accept that the next ten minutes are going to be kind of sucky, and simply let the anxiety wash over you.

And often, that's really the best thing you can do. According to Gummer, "One of the most powerful things that you can do in the midst of a panic attack is to accept it ... Accept that it's there. Feel it completely ... Yes, it can get pretty nasty. But usually at the point when I feel like my whole being is going to explode from so much anxiety, something almost unimaginable happens: a release." That's because panic doesn't last long. It's important to remember that it'll be over soon, and that you will survive.

While panic attacks feel pretty awful, they aren't actually life threatening. So the next time you feel one coming on, try your hardest to channel the nervous energy elsewhere. In the best case scenario, you'll stop the panic in its tracks. In the worst case, you'll spend some time distracting yourself (and dancing around) until the panic fizzles out on its own. Either way, it will end, and you'll be able to go on with your day. I promise.

Tip Three: Anxiety Scams on the Internet

Anxiety scams abound on the Internet, with promises of quick cures for panic attacks, phobias, and other anxiety problems. When you feel desperate, when your daily life has been so disrupted by chronic anxiety that you're ready to try anything, it's very tempting to log on and buy the next product you see.

Maybe it will help. But there's a good chance that you won't get the promised results. The worse result then isn't even the money you spent, it's that you become less hopeful about ever solving the problem. So it's important to choose your self help tools carefully, and not just grab the first promise you see. Claire Weekes offered hope and help. All too often, anxiety scams offer hustle and hype. How can you tell the difference? How can you be an informed consumer of anxiety products? Most importantly, how can you find something that works?

Here are some tips;

Beware of quick, easy "cures"

Anxiety scams promise quick, easy results. They claim that the great majority of people who use it are "cured" of their anxiety. They suggest that the creators of the product have some special secret or insight which contains great power to help you, something that no one else has thought of. They often offer statistics which can't be verified, and testimonials from people who can't be located.

Anxiety disorders are solvable problems, and most people who struggle with them can overcome them. But recovery does take some work. If the promise sounds too good to be true, it's probably an anxiety scam.

Look for people with professional credentials

The Internet is full of programs created by people with no professional training in health care, psychology, or any relevant field. They're generally people whose skills are in marketing and advertising.

They often try to turn this to their advantage by pointing out that many physicians and therapists don't know very much about anxiety disorders. This is unfortunately true, but it doesn't mean that the answer is to turn to Internet marketers. The answer is to find better sources of professionally trained help, and materials written by people with the training and background to be helpful to you.

Be wary of affiliate programs

On the Internet, anxiety scams are usually marketed and sold through "affiliate programs". In an affiliate program, people with products to sell offer others the chance to sell the product through their own web site and keep a commission, typically 50-75% of the sale price.

It's quick, easy, and cheap to set up, and affiliates can make some money with little effort. Nobody has anything to lose...except the buyers. This is why you'll see hundreds of web sites for these products.

This marketing has become so organized that there's even a market for buying and selling the articles that affiliates use to promote these products. Affiliates themselves often don't know much about the product, and pay free lance writers to do the writing for them.

Check out these examples. Here's an ad seeking 9 articles on "fat loss, dog training, and anxiety attacks". How about this one - 25 articles needed, for which the buyer will pay $1.50 each, on the topics of "hemorrhoid care, learn spanish quick, and cures for panic attacks".

Everybody needs to make a living, but this isn't how I want to get my health care problems solved!

How can you tell if you're looking at a product sold by affiliates? Just google the name of the product. If google returns lots of web sites advertising the product, all fairly similar, and linking you back to the same site for purchase, that's an affiliate program you found.

Compare prices

Most of the best self-help books for anxiety disorders sell for less than $20. Anxiety products on the Internet are typically priced far higher than that, even though they're often only digital files which cost nothing to reproduce. These products usually range in cost from $60 to $100. The prices vary because they often offer a "special low price that expires today!"

You can buy a small shelf of books by Claire Weekes for less than what you would pay for one anxiety scam. Dr. Reid Wilson, Dr. David Burns, and Dr. Edmund Bourne all have written excellent self-help books which sell for less than $20.

When the price seems really inflated, odds are it's an anxiety scam.

Seek information, not just advertising

A good self-help site will freely offer actual information that you can use. It probably has products for sale as well, but that isn't its only purpose. It will offer actual self-help information about anxiety disorders, and give you a clear idea of how the products can help you. The typical anxiety scam web site consists of screen after screen of high pressure reasons to buy, and lots of extras if you buy NOW. However, they rarely describe how their product actually works, or give you anything you can use. They just urge you to buy.

If you read through an entire web site and still can't tell what method the author proposes for you to use, odds are you're looking at an anxiety scam.

See if it's available elsewhere

The Internet is a wonderful medium. But why aren't these products also sold in stores, and large outlets like amazon? It's often because the product isn't good enough to get approval from third parties like editors, publishers, and retail distributors.

If these products were sold in stores, they'd attract a lot more scrutiny. Reviews would appear in newspapers and magazines. Customers would thumb through the books on shelves. Some Internet marketers don't want this kind of attention. Their strategy relies on catching you when you feel needy - maybe when you can't sleep and you're desperately surfing the Internet for help - and get you to make that impulse buy when you're least prepared to make a careful, considered choice.

When you can only get it from one supplier, the odds go up that it's an anxiety scam.

I have so much trouble - isn't it worth a try?

It might be. These products are generally overpriced and over promised, but that doesn't mean there's never anything of value. You might get something out of it, even if it's only a placebo.

But it's not a good place to start. A better way to start might be to go to amazon.com and search for books about the problem you face. Read about the authors, read the reviews, and you can often read a sample of the work itself. The odds of getting useful help from books you find that way are much, much higher than just googling the topic.

If you do want to try out an Internet product, then investigate it as best you can, and take two more simple steps.

Don't buy groceries when you're hungry

If you've ever struggled to control your diet and your weight, you probably have heard this suggestion. Don't go to the grocery store when you're hungry and grab whatever appeals to you. Instead, make a shopping list when you're not hungry, and follow that plan when you go to the store. That way, you can shop in an organized manner, rather than impulsively.

Tip Four: The Anxiety Trick

The Anxiety Trick is behind most of the trouble people have with chronic anxiety. Have you struggled to overcome an anxiety disorder, only to get disappointing results, or even feel worse over time? You're being fooled by the Anxiety Trick.

This is a terribly common occurrence, and people mistakenly blame themselves for it. Here's a more accurate, and helpful, way to understand this common and frustrating problem.

What is an anxiety disorder? It's you getting tricked into feeling powerful fear in the absence of any danger.

It's because there's no danger that people seek help for these fears. People recognize that they're getting afraid when they're not in danger. If they were actually in danger, they would just protect themselves as best they could, and be better off for it.

With an anxiety disorder, people get afraid when they're not in danger. Their struggle to protect themselves from fear leads them down a path of increasing trouble. That's the anxiety trick.

How does this happen, that you feel fear in the absence of danger? This is the Anxiety Trick at work.

How You Get Tricked

* If you have Panic Disorder or Agoraphobia, you

keep getting tricked into believing that you're about to die, go crazy, or lose control of yourself.

* If you have Social Phobia, you keep getting tricked into into believing that you're about to look so unreasonably nervous in front of people that you will be completely humiliated and be cast aside by your community.

* If you have a Specific Phobia, you keep getting tricked into believing that you're likely to be overcome by some external object (like an elevator) or animal, or by your fear of it.

* If you have OCD, you keep getting tricked into believing that you've set in motion a terrible calamity. You might fear that your neighborhood will burn because you left the stove on, or that your family will get poisoned because you mishandled the insecticide.

* If you have Generalized Anxiety Disorder, you keep getting tricked into believing that you're about to be driven mad by constant worrying.

In each case, the episode of fear passes without the expected catastrophe. You're none the worse for wear, except that you're more worried about the next episode. The details seem different, but it's the same anxiety trick.

What is the Anxiety Trick?

The Anxiety Trick is this: You experience Discomfort, and get fooled into treating it like Danger.

What do we do when we're in danger? We only have three things: Fight, Flight, and Freeze. If it looks weaker than me, I'll fight it. If it looks stronger than me, but slower, I'll run away. And if it looks stronger and faster than me, I'll freeze and hope it doesn't see so good. That's all we have for danger.

When people experience the fear of a panic attack, or a phobic encounter, or an obsessive thought, they instinctively treat it as a danger. They try to protect themselves, with some variation of Fight, Flight, or Freeze.

How People Get Tricked

People's natural instincts to protect themselves are what lead them to get tricked. See if you recognize your responses in these examples below.

A person with Panic Disorder gets tricked into holding her breath and fleeing the store (highway, theater, or other locale), rather than shifting to Belly Breathing. and staying there until the feelings pass.

A person with Generalized Anxiety Disorder gets tricked into trying to stop the unwanted "what if?" thoughts, rather than accepting them and taking care of present business as thoughts come and go.

A person with Social Phobia gets tricked into avoiding the party, or hiding in the corner if he attends, rather than say hello to a stranger and see what happens.

A person with OCD gets tricked into repeatedly washing his hands, or returning home to check the stove, rather than accepting the intrusive thoughts of contamination and fire and returning his energies to the present activities at hand.

A person with a dog phobia gets tricked into

avoiding the feelings by avoiding all dogs, rather than spending time with a dog until the feelings pass.

What Maintains the Anxiety Trick?

You might wonder, why don't people come to see this pattern, of repeated episodes of fear which don't lead to the feared outcome, and gradually lose their fear?

The answer is this. They took these protective steps, and there was no catastrophe. They tend to believe that these steps "saved" them from a catastrophe. This thought makes them worry more about "the next time". It convinces them that they are terribly vulnerable and must constantly protect themselves.

The actual reason they didn't experience a catastrophe is that such catastrophes are typically not part of a fear or phobia. These are anxiety disorders, not catastrophe disorders. People get through the experience because the experience isn't actually dangerous. But it's understandably hard for people to recognize that at the time. They're more likely to think they just had a "narrow escape". This leads them to redouble their protective steps.

It's the protective steps which actually maintain and strengthen the Anxiety Trick. If you think you just narrowly escaped a catastrophe because you had your cellular phone, or a water bottle; or because you went back and checked the stove seven times; or because you plugged in your iPod and distracted yourself with some music, then you're going to continue to feel vulnerable. And you're going to get more stuck in the habit of "protecting" yourself by these means.

This is how the problem gets embedded in your life. You think you're helping yourself, but you've actually been tricked into making it worse. That's how sneaky this Trick is.

This is why my patients so often say, "the harder I try, the worse it gets". If the harder you try, the worse it gets, then you should take another look at the methods you've been using. You've probably been tricked into trying to protect yourself against something that isn't dangerous, and this makes your fear worse over time.

How Can You Overcome The Anxiety Trick?

The thing that makes fears and phobias so persistent is that virtually anything you do to oppose, escape, or distract from the anxious feelings and thoughts will be turned against you, and make the anxiety a more persistent part of your life.

This is why people notice "the harder I try, the worse it gets". They're putting out fires with gasoline.

If you come to see that you've been putting out fires with gasoline, you may not have any idea what to do next. But the first step is always the same: put down the buckets. Stop throwing gasoline on that fire.

This is where the cognitive behavioral methods of desensitization and exposure come in. They're intended as methods by which you can practice with (not against) the symptoms, and become less sensitive to them. As you lose your fear of the symptoms, through this practice, that's when the symptoms will fade.

All too often, people get the idea that exposure means going to a place or situation where you're likely to get anxious, perhaps a highway or an elevator, and take a ride without getting anxious. That's not the point! The point is to actually go there and feel the anxiety, being sure to stay there and letting the anxiety leave first. This is what Claire Weekes called floating.

The way to disarm the Anxiety Trick is to increasingly spend time with anxiety, to expose yourself to the thoughts and sensations, and allow them to subside over time.

What can you do to make the experience of exposure more tolerable? You can use the AWARE steps as a general guide for how to conduct yourself while doing exposure. Always keep in mind that exposure is practice with fear, and do nothing to oppose, avoid, or distract from the fear during exposure.